AT DEATH'S DOOR

Jasper Newton Hall

AT DEATH'S DOOR

A Yankee Soldier's Story of Survival in Confederate Captivity

Edited by Richard A. Baumgartner

Richard A. Baumgartner 28 June 2014

BLUE ACORN PRESS

Blue Acorn Press
P.O. Box 2684
Huntington, W.Va. 25726 USA

ISBN 978-1-885033-37-6

Hall, Jasper Newton, 1835 – 1916

Baumgartner, Richard A., 1953 –

 *At Death's Door: A Yankee Soldier's
Story of Survival in Confederate Captivity*

Illustrated.
Includes bibliographical references and index.

History — U.S. Civil War, 1861-1865 — Personal narratives.

Manufactured in the United States of America

In memory of all prisoners of war,
North and South,
who survived, and those who did not.

Contents

Acknowledgments

Sincere gratitude is extended to those who assisted in this book's background research, especially Anne Billeter, director of the Rogue Valley Genealogical Society & Jackson County Genealogy Library, Phoenix, Oregon; Carolyn Johnson Burns, genealogist at the Veterans Administration Medical Center, Dayton, Ohio; and John Gray, cemetery administrator, Andersonville National Historic Site, Andersonville, Georgia. For photographic contributions, appreciation is due Larry M. Strayer of Dayton, Ohio; Richard W. Fink of Kenton, Ohio; and Michael C. Wright of Monticello, Indiana. Lastly, I am particularly indebted to my good friend Dennis M. Keesee of Westerville, Ohio, for the loan of Francis M. McAdams' published history of the 113th Ohio Infantry Regiment, and providing original issues of Urbana, Ohio, wartime newspapers.

Introduction

During the late afternoon of September 20, 1863, in a wooded ravine on the shot-torn battlefield of Chickamauga, Georgia, Sergeant Jasper Hall's life forever changed.

He had escaped injury in this, his very first battle, his body untouched by whining bullets or flying fragments of artillery shells. But like more than 4,000 fellow soldiers clad in dusty, sweat-stained blue uniforms at Chickamauga, he was a prisoner — unluckily caught between opposing lines of fire and helplessly unable to evade enemy capture. For Sergeant Hall, that evening marked the beginning of 585 days he remained a Confederate captive — more than 19 months of deprivation, sickness and suffering which several times brought him to death's door. He considered his unlikely survival nothing short of miraculous, as did friends and family when he finally returned home in the summer of 1865, a physical shadow of his former self.

Like scorbutic sores gnawing at his flesh, Hall's prison memories remained unforgettably vivid long afterward, so much so that he finished recording them on paper about the year 1880. Unlike embellished, exaggerated and often inaccurate accounts written postwar by a number of former Civil War prison inmates, Hall's narrative was straight-forward, surprisingly dispassionate and remarkably free of rancor toward his captors, with one or two exceptions.

Born to farmers Thomas R. and Maria Bousman Hall on October 1, 1835, Jasper Newton Hall grew up near the hamlet of Carysville, Ohio, among the gently rolling, agriculturally rich hills of northwest Champaign County. For nearly 30 years two generations of his forebears had farmed in the county's Concord Township; grandfather John

Hall emigrated there from Patrick County, Virginia, in 1806, and father Thomas R. Hall, born in 1811, tilled the soil for many years in both Concord and Adams townships. His first wife, Maria, gave birth to five children, including Jasper, prior to her death in 1844. Thomas remarried in 1846 and fathered seven more children.[1]

Jasper Hall passed his formative years assisting on the family farm while attending local country schools. At an early age he acquired a keen aptitude for reading and, with a predilection for study whenever farm chores didn't interfere, eventually landed a seasonal teaching job in Carysville by the time he turned 18.

In 1859 he began boarding with Carysville shoemaker and part-time preacher Rockwell H. Seely, an association that would last for much of the next two decades. Staunch Douglas Democrats, both men apprehensively watched the country's sectional differences slide ominously toward open, armed conflict. When it finally occurred in April 1861 with the Confederate bombardment of Fort Sumter in Charleston harbor, South Carolina, Hall, flushed with patriotic fervor, left Carysville to enlist in the Union army. At the nearby town of Sidney in Shelby County, he joined the 20th Ohio Volunteer Infantry and immediately was appointed a corporal in Company H. This regiment mustered for three months' service, which it primarily spent marching and performing guard duty along the Baltimore & Ohio Railroad in western Virginia. By the time the 20th's enlistment term expired that August, it sustained 10 fatal casualties — three by accidents and seven from disease.[2]

Hall returned to Champaign County and resumed boarding with shoemaker Seely, whose teen-aged daughter Florence already had caught the ex-soldier's eye. The two courted for the next 10 months while Hall employed himself by farming and teaching.[3]

In the meantime the war dragged on. With ever-increasing demands for more manpower prompted by the failure of General George B. McClellan's Peninsula campaign and Union reverses in Virginia's Shenandoah Valley, President Abraham Lincoln's July 1862 call to raise 300,000 additional troops rekindled recruiting efforts in the Buckeye State. More than 58,000 Ohioans responded to the call, including nearly 700 from Franklin, Licking, Madison, Logan and Champaign counties destined for the 113th Ohio Infantry Regiment. Among them was Jasper Hall, who reenlisted August 16 in the western Champaign village of St. Paris. The next day he was followed by 48-year-old Rockwell Seely, who earlier in 1862 had been elected Adams Township assessor. On August 24 he became Hall's father-in-law when Jasper and Florence were married at Westville, Ohio.[4]

Just as quickly the newlyweds were separated. On the 28th at the county seat of Urbana, Hall and Mr. Seely boarded a train bound for Camp Chase in Columbus. There, along with 90 other recruits from Champaign County assigned to Company E, the pair contemplated its new comrades, surroundings and futures. Commented the *Ohio State Journal* on August 29: "This is the oldest looking company we have seen. We noticed several gray-haired men. This is all right, and there is more of deliberate valor and bravery to be expected from men of riper years. The company joins the 113th regiment." Three days later Hall, a month shy of his 27th birthday, was selected Company E's 4th sergeant, while his father-in-law was appointed 4th corporal.[5]

Living in tents at Camp Chase, the 113th spent eight weeks drilling and absorbing the rudiments of guard and fatigue duty. Uniforms were received September 18, and on the 29th Enfield rifle muskets, cartridge boxes and belts were issued. "We begin to look like soldiers," proclaimed a Company E private proudly.[6]

On October 25 the regiment moved to Muskingum County's Camp Zanesville, and was greeted by an early-season snowfall three inches deep. Upon reaching Zanesville one of Hall's company comrades, Private Francis M. McAdams, wrote that "we found ourselves with more appetite than rations." He somewhat gleefully observed that, once in camp outside town, "the boys commenced an indiscriminate slaughter on some swine, which, unfortunately for their owner, had strayed within the lines. Only eleven of them fell sacrifices to our voracious appetites, and half a dozen of the boys fared sumptuously at the guard-house in consequence."[7]

Within three weeks of arrival at Zanesville (which McAdams described as "a dingy, smoky looking place, much larger than Urbana, but will not compare with it in appearance"), the regiment's billets in large, well ventilated wooden buildings went up in smoke. A fire of undetermined origin broke out in one of the barracks the morning of November 10 while the regiment was out drilling. "The flames spread rapidly from house to house," McAdams noted, "and in an hour the main part of the camp was in ashes." Although no one was killed or seriously injured, he surmised "The losses sustained by the enlisted men of several of the companies prove to be great. Many a pack of cards, several violins and some other outfits of amusement will have to be replaced." By November 17, however, the construction of temporary new quarters had been completed.[8]

Training at Camp Zanesville continued until mid-December, when the 113th entrained for Camp Dennison outside Cincinnati. There, Company I was added from fractional elements of the 109th Ohio, which failed to organize. Writing from Dennison on December 22, Private McAdams summed up his comrades' sentiments by extolling qualities of their regimental commander:

> Col. [James A.] Wilcox has been assiduous and untiring in his efforts to complete the regiment, and prepare it for active service, and had the 113th been in charge of a man of less indomitable energy than his, it might not to-day claim the praise that it does. For all his labor and pains the Col. is rewarded by knowing that he has the confidence of his men, and a regiment for drill and discipline surpassed by none that was ever organized in Ohio. We believe his fighting qualities have never been tested, but if his go-aheadativeness in the field equals what it has been, his men are ready to trust him, and willing to go at his command.[9]

By New Year's Eve the 113th, now nine companies strong, unexpectedly found itself "in Dixie" after a steamboat ride down the Ohio River to Louisville, Kentucky. It soon "received praise for its orderly conduct and soldierly bearing." But as anxious as the Ohioans were to come to grips with the enemy, their initial service at the front began in mundane fashion — performing guard duty on the Louisville & Nashville Railroad 36 miles south of Louisville. While the soldiers groused, the *Ohio State Journal* editorialized: "This is hardly the responsible work that should be assigned to Cols. Wilcox and Mitchell and Major Warner. They are brave, daring officers, and command *fighting* men. Give them a chance."[10]

Despite the *Journal's* stance, during the first five months of 1863 the 113th Ohio battled snow drifts in Kentucky and blisters at Frank-

A Columbus native and attorney born in 1828, Colonel James A. Wilcox commanded the 113th Ohio from its organization until his resignation April 29, 1863. He later served as acting assistant provost marshal general at Columbus, and was brevetted brigadier general in late 1865.

Courtesy of Larry M. Strayer

lin, Tennessee, where, as part of the Army of the Cumberland's right wing, it participated in numerous foraging expeditions, several scouts and worked "almost incessantly" on extensive fortifications along the north bank of the Harpeth River. At the end of April Colonel Wilcox resigned, his position being filled by John G. Mitchell of Columbus, promoted from lieutenant colonel. On May 15 Company E's commander, Captain John F. Riker, also resigned and was replaced by one of Sergeant Hall's old acquaintances, John Bowersock, the co-owner of a mill and distillery back in St. Paris, Ohio.[11]

"I think we have a very nice, healthy camp here," wrote Hall's father-in-law, Rockwell Seely, from Franklin. It was "well supplied by water from the numerous springs in the vicinity, and the boys seemingly enjoy themselves as well as could be expected of soldiers." Still, Seely and his son-in-law, like most of the army's rank and file (as well as government officials in Washington), wondered when a forward move would be made.[12]

Finally, in the last week of June the Army of the Cumberland under Major General William S. Rosecrans departed its Murfreesboro-area camps and, in spite of drenching downpours, marched against General Braxton Bragg's Confederate Army of Tennessee. Over the next 11 days Rosecrans' maneuvering in the so-called Tullahoma campaign forced Bragg out of Middle Tennessee to refuge in Chattanooga. Belonging to the newly organized Cumberland army's Reserve Corps, the 113th Ohio reached Shelbyville, Tennessee, on June 30, having encountered no living enemy soldiers except for occasional parties of prisoners or deserters being marched rearward. The regiment remained at Shelbyville and nearby Wartrace for the following two months, guarding the Nashville & Chattanooga Railroad, drilling, foraging, picking blackberries and swimming in the Duck River. Cedar shade arbors were erected in front of officers' tents. For some this summer idyll seemed a "protracted picnic." [13]

Such bloodless service ended for Hall and his comrades on September 6, 1863, when the 113th left Wartrace — still untested in combat — and embarked on an arduous new campaign culminating a fortnight later in the ferocious battle of Chickamauga. It marched with Major General Gordon Granger's Reserve Corps in Brigadier General James B. Steedman's 1st Division, whose 2nd Brigade, led by Colonel John G. Mitchell, consisted of the 78th Illinois, 98th, 113th and 121st Ohio Infantry regiments, and Battery M, 1st Illinois Light Artillery.

Commanded by Lieutenant Colonel Darius B. Warner, the 113th's nine companies stormed up Horseshoe Ridge on September 20 with 355 officers and enlisted men. One hundred and nineteen were killed or wounded. Another 12 were captured or listed as missing. [14] Chickamauga "was a bloody baptism for the regiment," wrote historian and wartime journalist Whitelaw Reid. Lieutenant Colonel Warner concurred, adding, "The number of [our] killed and wounded on that day is all the testimony necessary as to their valor." [15]

For Jasper Hall, however, the battle's conclusion meant his ordeal was just beginning.

Richard A. Baumgartner
Huntington, West Virginia

Introduction Notes

1. Hall family genealogy can be found in *The History of Champaign County, Ohio* (Chicago: W.H. Beers & Co., 1881), p. 772, and on the Internet at http://www.heritagepursuit.com/Champaign. Jasper Hall was first-born; two of his siblings died in infancy.

2. Jasper N. Hall compiled service record, 20th Ohio three-months' service 1861, Record Group (RG) 94, National Archives & Records Administration (NARA), Washington, D.C.; *Official Roster of the Soldiers of the State of Ohio in the War of the Rebellion, 1861-1866,* vol. I (Akron: The Werner Company, 1893), p. 407-408, 420; Frank Conover, editor, *Centennial Portrait and Biographical Record of the City of Dayton and of Montgomery County, Ohio* (Logansport, Ind.: A.W. Bowen & Co., 1897), p. 553; J.N. Hall pension application, claim #610254, RG 15, NARA.

3. Depositions of R.H. Seely and F.D. Hall in J.N. Hall pension application, claim #610254, RG 15, NARA. Rockwell Seely was a native of Seneca County, N.Y.

4. Whitelaw Reid, *Ohio in the War. Her Statesmen, Generals and Soldiers,* vol. II (Cincinnati: The Robert Clarke Company, 1895), p. 4; Steven H. Ward, *Buckeyes All. A Compendium and Bibliography of Ohio in the Civil War,* vol. V revised (Dayton: privately published, 2004), p. 744; J.N. Hall and R.H. Seely compiled service records, 113th Ohio, RG 94, NARA; F.D. Hall deposition in J.N. Hall pension application, claim #610254, RG 15, NARA; *The History of Champaign County, Ohio,* p. 468. Upon enlistment, their company descriptive book listed Hall as five feet ten inches tall with fair complexion, hazel eyes and dark hair, while Rockwell Seely stood five foot seven with auburn hair and blue eyes.

5. Francis M. McAdams, *Every-Day Soldier Life, or a History of the One Hundred and Thirteenth Ohio Volunteer Infantry* (Columbus: M. Cott & Co., 1884), p. 5-6; *Ohio State Journal,* August 29, 1862; J.N. Hall and R.H. Seely compiled service records, RG 94, NARA. For almost a year and a half the 113th Ohio remained an incomplete organization. Companies H and I joined the regiment in December 1862, while Company K finally was mustered in February 29, 1864, at Camp Rossville, Ga.

6. McAdams, p. 8-14.

7. F.M. McAdams, November 3, 1862, to the *Urbana Citizen and Gazette,* November 6, 1862.

8. F.M. McAdams, November 10, 1862, to the *Urbana Citizen and Gazette,* November 13, 1862; McAdams, p. 11-12.

9. F.M. McAdams, December 22, 1862, to the *Urbana Citizen and Gazette*, January 1, 1863.

10. McAdams, p. 14; Reid, vol. II, p. 595; excerpt from *Ohio State Journal* editorial in the *Urbana Union*, January 21, 1863.

11. Reid, vol. II, p. 595; *Ohio Rosters*, vol. VIII (Cincinnati: The Ohio Valley Press, 1888), p. 77, 89; J. Bowersock compiled service record, RG 94, NARA. Company E's original first lieutenant, Bowersock, 25, mustered as captain on June 7, 1863. He was killed in action June 27, 1864, during the 113th Ohio's unsuccessful assault at the Dead Angle near Kennesaw Mountain, Ga. Earlier in the war, John G. Mitchell had served as adjutant of the 3rd Ohio Infantry Regiment, then as captain of Company C.

When Captain Riker returned home, he discovered Champaign County broiling in the heat of political discord. Statewide, a contentious gubernatorial campaign between Union Party candidate John Brough and Peace Democrat Clement L. Vallandigham was in full swing. Vallandigham, a former state legislator and U.S. congressman, was among the most virulent, outspoken critics of the Lincoln administration and widely known "Copperheads" publicly espousing factious opposition to the Federal government. Imprisoned for his speeches, he was banished to the Confederacy by Lincoln in late May 1863. Confederate authorities likewise ejected him from the South, whereupon Vallandigham moved to Canada and continued his political campaign from there.

These events, slave emancipation and the prolonged war polarized many Ohio citizens, especially in Champaign County. Letters and newspaper accounts of "Copperhead" agitation in Adams Township aroused the ire of soldiers like Jasper Hall and his father-in-law, Rockwell Seely, who fairly regularly received the county's two largest weeklies in their Tennessee camps. Although a lifelong Democrat, the opinionated Seely nonetheless supported Northern military aims and condemned what he perceived as subversive rhetoric and activity by some of the township's officials and his neighbors near Carysville. On May 31 he vented with unrestrained disdain to the *Urbana Citizen and Gazette:*

"Many of those persons have turned traitors to their country, and while we have the rebels of the south in our front, they are firing in the rear. ... It would be better for those traitors to have a millstone hanged about their necks, and they cast into the depths of the sea, than to offend the soldiers or their families. ... Silly Copperheads, they have sold their rights for a pot of cabbage, and lost all rights to citizenship. But I, with some of them in former days mingled my voice in church, and on politics, with pleasure, and while I still maintain my integrity to my God, and to my country, they have, like the sow, turned to her wallowing in the mire. If you do not return, we will not claim you as Democrats, for a good true Democrat is for the *Union,* let it cost what it will.

"Well did the Hon. Stephen A. Douglas say, that there were but two parties, *Union* and *Disunion.* It cannot be otherwise. We must serve God or the Devil. This half way business is played out. You may think I talk plain, and so I do. ... But I wish my friends to know how I stand on the war. I am not fighting to free the negro. I am fighting to save our once happy country from the hands of the vilest traitors. I believe that every soldier feels it his duty to let the nigger question and politics rest until the war is over. Let such matters sink with stigma, with Vallandigham and his followers. ... Let me say to [my friends at home] through the paper: You will not suffer. You have shed many tears for some loved ones in the army. Some will no doubt never return; yet if they fall, they fall in a good cause. Although the Copperheads may hiss their venom at you — tell you that you are disgraced because your husband or son is in the army — let me tell you that the soldiers are looking forward to the day when honor will be put upon them to whom honor is due." [R.H. Seely, May 31, 1863, in the *Urbana Citizen and Gazette,* June 18, 1863].

Divisive tension between opposing sides in Adams Township remained high during the summer of 1863, finally exploding August 20 following a Union meeting and rally held a half mile south of Carysville. As a procession of singing Unionists carrying flags and banners entered Main Street in 16 wagons and buggies, it was attacked by some 150 screaming "Vallandighammers" armed with stones, brickbats and several guns. An eyewitness claimed 100 shots rang out before the firing ceased and the rioters dispersed. One Unionist was fatally wounded, while seven Vallandigham supporters soon were arrested or gave themselves up. Newspaper editor Joshua Saxton commented: "The attack upon the Union men was entirely unprovoked, and exhibits a bad state of feeling among the Copperheads of Adams township. ... Such scoundrels need attention, and the sooner they are taught better manners the better it will be for all concerned." [*Urbana Citizen and Gazette,* August 27, 1863].

12. R.H. Seely, May 31, 1863, to the *Urbana Citizen and Gazette,* June 18, 1863.

13. McAdams, p. 31-37.

14. *The War of the Rebellion: A Compilation of the Official Records of the Union and Confederate Armies,* series I, vol. XXX, pt. 1, p. 46, 178, 858. (Hereafter referred to as *Official Records*); McAdams, p. 38, 40; Reid, vol. II, p. 596. Colonel Mitchell, 113th Ohio, took command of the 2nd Brigade on September 15.

15. Reid, vol. II, p. 596; D.B. Warner quoted in McAdams, p. 351.

1

Chickamauga

Suffering the pangs of defeat and surrender

In writing the following narrative of prison life, I shall begin at the battle at which I was captured, the bloody field of Chickamauga, which was fought on the 19th and 20th of September 1863.[1]

We had been following the rebel army under Bragg all the way from Shelbyville to Chattanooga, and had about given up hope of his giving us battle. Our corps, under General Gordon Granger, had pitched tents near Rossville, an insignificant village near five miles south of Chattanooga, and was now resting from the tiresome marches of several days previous. On the third day after our halt, the division (Steedman's) to which we were attached started on a reconnaissance in the direction of Ringgold and Tunnel Hill, a distance of nearly twenty miles from our camp.[2] The Confederates were reported to be in that direction with a strong force, and the object of our movement was to ascertain his position and strength.

Late in the afternoon, and within three miles of Ringgold, we encountered the outposts of the enemy, driving them in and appropriating their half-cooked supper of yams and sweet potatoes, which we found cooking in iron kettles.

Halting about a mile from town, we placed six pieces of artillery in a commanding position and, for a time, paid our compliments to our enemies after the cast-iron fashion.[3] I was sent with a squad of men to the top of a hill on our left to ascertain and report any aggressive demonstration of the foe, but nothing occurred of importance. Our division, having accomplished the object of the trip, began to fall back toward Rossville late in the evening, and I was ordered to move in the rear with my squad. The Confederates, ascertaining that we were falling back, pressed our rear, and for several miles and until darkness came on, a brisk skirmish fight was kept up, in which our loss was

Licking County enlisted men of Company D, 113th Ohio, photographed circa 1863. All wear four-button fatigue blouses and large brass company letters adorn four of their army-issue hats.

three killed and eight or ten wounded. We had now reached a scope of heavy timber and were permitted to move on unmolested. Coming at length to a level piece of bottom land, through which runs the stream Chickamauga, we forded the stream and went into camp on the edge of the prairie near a strip of timber. It was now nearly ten o'clock at night, and our camp fires were soon blazing in the necessary preparations for supper and rest.

During the afternoon I had had the misfortune to lose my darkey who carried my haversack and blankets, but Captain Bowersock generously shared with me his rations and, supper being over, we stretched ourselves on the ground with our feet to the fire, congratulating ourselves that we might rest for the remainder of the night. Our enemies had calculated otherwise, for, just as Morpheus was escorting us into the dim land of dreams, we were startled by the report of a cannon shot, and the whiz of a shell filled the air above our heads. This was followed by others in rapid succession, until the air seemed alive with screaming, screeching, exploding, deadly missiles. To spring to our feet, seize our arms and extinguish our fires was but the work of a few seconds. All was confusion for a time, but, changing our position for another that seemed to promise security, we again lay down and rested unmolested till dawn.[4]

Returning to the vicinity of Rossville, our former camp, we remained the greater part of the day, and being within a few miles of the battle, which opened early in the morning, we could hear the roar of cannon and the din of battle as it progressed. This was Saturday, September 19th, the first day of the conflict. None of us comprehended the extent of the engagement now pending, nor did we realize that the day and the morrow would be fraught with the mighty events that have since passed into history.

About dusk we received orders to march immediately and, leaving our tents and personal effects in charge of a light guard, we were soon moving at a quick pace in the direction of Chickamauga Creek and the fatal field. At the distance of six miles we halted and spent the night without fires, though the night was frosty and cold.

The sun had scarcely risen the next (Sunday) morning when the opening roar of cannon to the southeast of us told that the bloody work of the day had begun. After a hurried breakfast we fell in line and advanced about two miles to the east, where we halted and threw out a line of pickets. As the day advanced the roar of cannon became incessant, and the noise of musketry was a deafening accompaniment. We could see the sulphur smoke of battle, and its locality indicated to us the position of the deadly combatants. We were all on the tip-toe of excitement; some seemed anxious to go forward and share in the struggle with the foe; others shrank and grew pale; but truth compels me to say that in the hours that followed, the timid and the bold fought with equal bravery.

About half past [eleven] o'clock the bugle called us to arms, and we were hurried at double quick toward the scene of battle. Presently we came to where the dead and wounded lay scattered over the field, the surgeons busy attending to the latter. This was a trying moment, for, as we were hurried along we crossed a level, open piece of ground, and the enemy appearing in the woods on our left, opened a deadly artillery fire upon us and, strange as it may appear, our line crossed that space of several hundred yards and not a man was injured.

Striking the timber again we came very nearly entering the enemy's lines. General Steedman rode up, his horse covered with a heavy lather of sweat, and gave orders to file to the right. We hurried through a cornfield and took our position in the timber. Stray balls were flying around with a continual spatter. In five minutes after coming to a halt we were ordered to charge up the rising ground in our front. Obeying, we met the flying remnant of a regiment of our troops, who were being swept by the enemy from the position to which we were advancing; but on we went and, reaching the summit, we met the enemy in over-whelming numbers. Now came the tug of war. Grape, canister, shot, shell and other death-dealing projectiles made of our ranks a harvest of death, and in five minutes nearly one-fourth of our regiment was either killed or wounded.[5] Utter destruction awaited us. We wavered, gave way and fled down the hill in disorder. Reaching a somewhat sheltered position we halted and, re-forming, lay down in line of battle. Shells and cannon-balls were doing their deadly work, cutting trees and large branches which, in their fall, sent consternation and sometimes death into our ranks. One limb in its fall killed two men.

Our division was now occupying the brow of a hill with orders to hold it to the very last moment. The men hugged the ground, loading and firing continually, each man as fast as he could. The deafening roar of musketry and the boom of cannon drowned, in a great measure, the shrieks of the wounded and dying. Every moment was heard the dull thud which told that another had been killed or wounded. A few yards to my right stood a man behind a tree a foot in diameter. He was loading and firing at will, intent on killing all he could. But the brave fellow's earthly career was cut short by a cannon ball which struck the tree four feet from the ground, cutting the tree off and killing the man so suddenly that he never knew how he was struck.

We held our position till nearly sundown. Nearly half the men in our company and the regiment were killed, wounded or missing, and at each successive moment our ranks were melting under the terrific fire which continued to assail us. We had done all that brave men could do to hold our position, and further stay here seemed like death to the re-mainder. At length an order was received to fall back, and the field with our gallant dead and wounded was left to the foe. After proceeding a short distance I turned aside in company with a comrade of Company B, and, as we again turned to run and rejoin our retreating column, he was struck by a ball and instantly killed. I caught him in my arms and laid him on the ground. Being unable to render him any assistance in his last moments, except at the risk of my life, I again ran forward.[6]

As I ran down the hill I came near to a poor fellow whose leg had just been shot away midway between the knee and foot. He begged me for God's sake to stop, and though the balls were flying thick and fast, I could not refuse him. I tied up his leg as well as I could and, as I rose to run again, my canteen dropped to the ground. Stooping to pick it up I noticed that the strap was cut asunder by a ball, and this made me decide to let the canteen take care of itself, and I hurried forward as fast as I could run.

Reaching the gulch at the foot of the hill, I discovered that our forces had been reenforced, or had been able to re-form, and were now in position on the opposite side of the gulch on the high ground, and were opening fire on the advancing rebels. This placed me under the fire of friend and foe, and doubled my danger.

Two others, left by their commands, were trying to find shelter behind a double tree which grew in the gulch. While I argued with them that there was room for a third, one of them was shot through the hips. I then concluded that I did not want the place, and at once started down the gulch hoping to reach a place of safety by flanking friend and foe.

I plunged into the thick undergrowth, feeling that I had hopes of escape, but I ran right into a regiment of Confederates lying concealed in the brush. A half dozen muskets were pointed at me, and I was ordered to surrender. I had no alternative to do otherwise, and accepted the situation.

I saw that the regiment or brigade into whose midst I had run was bent on some particular object, for it was creeping along cautiously and lying close to the ground. I asked my captors if I might stand behind a tree, which would shelter me from the fire of our own troops; being a prisoner, I did not wish to be killed by my friends. To this they consented, and for a brief time a friendly oak protected me. The balls from our troops were flying dangerously near, and the dead and wounded of both armies were to be seen all around me. At length there came a momentary lull in the firing, but this was followed by a storm of shot, shell and musketry poured into the ranks of the rebels by the Union troops, almost annihilating them. They fell back, leaving large numbers of their dead and wounded, and also leaving me behind the tree to care for myself. I hesitated how to proceed, but concluded to pursue my flight down the gulch in the bare hope of finding an open space through which I might escape the foe and rejoin my retreating friends. I had proceeded but a short distance when I ran into a second line of the enemy, and was again a prisoner.

It was now sundown, and the work of that bloody Sabbath was drawing to a close; the fighting ceased to be general and the enemy at once took the best means of securing the hard-earned fruits of the day's conflict. I was hurried to the rear and joined a squad of near two hundred other prisoners, and as night came on we remained on the field under a strong guard.

I dare not recall the feelings that robbed me of slumber during that long night. I would not recall them if I could. One of the most painful recollections of one who has gone through a battle is that of his friends lying wounded and dying, and who need that help which he is utterly unable to give. I suffered this and much more for, as the weary hours wore away, the pangs of defeat and the consciousness that we had fallen into the hands of a merciless enemy added to the terror of our situation.

The next morning most of the Union prisoners who were not wounded were set to the work of caring for the wounded Union troops who, being unable to leave the field, had fallen into the hands of the rebels. Nearly all the wounded of both armies were yet on the field, and in general uncared for. There was a vast number of each class, and the work of collecting them together and giving the necessary attention to each man was a task a hundredfold greater than could be performed. This was Monday morning, and the battle had raged for the two days before over an area of fields and woods several miles in extent.

We prisoners were permitted to care for our wounded as best we could, but the most we could do for them was to bring them water and give them such acts of attention as our limited means afforded. Hundreds died who, with proper medical attention in time, might

Jasper Newton Hall, as he appeared about the time
he wrote his prison memoir in 1880.

have lived and recovered. It is probably due to our foes to say that their time was fully employed in the care of their own wounded, and that the inattention given to ours was a necessity and beyond their control. We collected fifty or more of our comrades together and placed them in an old house and shed adjoining. This house and its surroundings showed many evidences of the conflict, as several holes were to be seen in it which had been made by cannon-balls. It stood in what had been a cornfield, but the fences and the crop and nearly everything but the naked house and the ground on which it stood had been swept away by the battle.

Besides this house there were numbers of other places on various parts of the field of battle where our wounded were collected and cared for by the well prisoners, if such attention as we were able to give them might be called care and attention. By Tuesday, after Sunday's battle, we had many more wounded on our hands than we could possibly attend to, and many perished for lack of attention. The rebels were still busy attending *their* wounded and burying *their* dead; our dead being as yet unburied, the work of decay had set in and the stench produced thereby was insufferable. This state of affairs made the condition of our unfortunate comrades the more deplorable, for to be compelled to inhale the tainted atmosphere was, of itself, horrible.

The family who owned the house we were occupying, and who had been driven from it by the battle, returned on Tuesday following the battle. Everything of a personal character, except the house, had been destroyed or swept away by the contending armies, and the situation upon the return of the family was anything but inviting and agreeable. The old lady, a tall, angular woman with a Roman nose and dark, penetrating eyes, was fired with malicious rage toward the Yankees. Coming into the house and finding the floor covered with the suffering wounded, she gave vent to her feelings in a tirade which I shall never wish to hear repeated, and which I can never forget. "Oh, you wretches," said she, "I am glad to hear you groan. If I durst, I would set fire to the house and burn it over your heads." And I think she would have done so but for fear of the guards who, I must say, treated us kindly. A brave soldier, let him fight on whatever side he may, is always magnanimous and merciful to his captive. It is the dastard and coward who uses this opportunity to inflict upon his helpless captive a humiliation or insult.

On Wednesday, September 23d, I got permission to go over that part of the battlefield on which the 113th had fought on Sunday afternoon, thinking I might find some of my comrades of the regiment who were yet alive, and to whom I might be of some service. I found every bush and tree bearing the marks of the conflict; every object was marked with grape, cannon and rifle balls; even the small twigs had been cut down and the forest appeared as though a mighty whirlwind had swept through it. I counted on one tree the marks of forty shots, and the wonder is that any man could stand in such a place and live for a moment.

I found our dead here and there, lying where they fell — sometimes singly, sometimes in groups, all unburied. I recognized the faces of a number of the 113th among the dead. Many of the wounded were yet alive, but all I could do for the poor fellows was to give them a drink of water. Captain Joshua M. Wells, Company C, 113th O.V.I., was still alive, having been shot through the left lung. He was fully conscious and expressed hopes of recovery. Giving what attention I could, I returned to our hospital at the old house, and giving an old man two dollars I had the Captain brought in and placed where I could give him attention. Here I gave him all possible care, but under the circumstances very little extra care could be bestowed upon a single one.

Captain Wells lived till the following Sunday, September 27th, and met death like a heroic Christian soldier. While I attended him he expressed a great desire that his body should be sent home to his family at Columbus, O., in case of his death. I assured him it should be done if possible, but I felt utterly powerless to do so. The Captain's body was laid in a grave prepared by my hands; I also marked his grave by a headboard, cutting thereon his name, company and regiment. I afterward wrote to his widow, giving her an account of the incidents of his closing hours and of the sad rites I had performed. Some months later, when the Federal troops obtained possession of the battlefield, the body was exhumed and sent home in a good state of preservation.[7]

For a week following the Captain's death we remained in this place, continually burdened with the care of the wounded and the burial of the dead. Up to this time, fourteen days after the conflict, the dead were not all buried and the stench arising from the decaying bodies surpassed all description, and I am inclined to think caused the speedy deaths of many of our wounded.

An exchange of wounded prisoners on both sides was now effected by and between General Rosecrans and General Bragg.[8] We prisoners who had remained thus in care of the sick had allowed ourselves to hope that we would be included in the exchange. But we were doomed to disappointment, for on the day following we were mustered into line, our names, companies and regiments listed, and then marched to a station on the railroad between Chattanooga and Ringgold, where we were loaded in box cars, dozens of men to each car, and sent south to Atlanta. Remaining two days at Atlanta, we were again loaded on a train and sent to Richmond, Va., arriving at our destination about the 10th or 12th of October 1863.[9]

Chickamauga Notes

1. Hall's account originally was written about 1880. Entitled "Prison Life. A Story of Capture, Imprisonment and Suffering in Rebel Prisons of the South," it appeared in Francis M. McAdams' history of the 113th Ohio published in 1884 (pages 267-331), and as a separate publication with the same title later that year. Hall and McAdams served together in Company E. Between August and December 1891, Hall's "Nineteen Months in Rebel Hell" — substantially the same narrative as "Prison Life" — was serialized over eight issues of Volume 5 in *The Ohio Soldier and National Picket Guard.*

For ease of reading here, original misspellings, typographical errors and some punctuation have been corrected. Chapter and more frequent paragraph breaks also have been added, as well as a number of photographs.

2. Steedman's division of the Reserve Corps marched from Bridgeport, Ala., at 7 a.m. on September 13 and reached Rossville, Ga. — a distance of nearly 40 miles — at 11 a.m. the next day. The Ringgold reconnaissance began on September 17 at 3 a.m. [*Official Records,* series I, vol. XXX, pt. 1, p. 859].

3. Generals Granger and Steedman both reported that only one section of artillery was used to drive the Confederates out of Ringgold. [*Official Records,* series I, vol. XXX, pt. 1, p. 853, 859].

4. *Ibid.,* p. 859. Six shells were fired into Steedman's camps before the Confederates withdrew.

5. Hall's first lieutenant, Joseph Swisher, recalled that "When the conflict was raging the hottest, three men of Company E, all red headed — namely: Thomas Scott, David Chatfield and Frank[lin] Russell — were charging on the rebel hosts, when I heard Scott make the remark that 'us red-headed fellows could stand it as well as any,' when, at the same instant, Russell was killed, Scott was wounded and Chatfield had his blanket riddled with bullets." Three days after the battle the blanket, perforated with 49 holes, passed around the 113th Ohio's Chattanooga camp as a curiosity. [McAdams, p. 43, 335].

Company E's casualties on September 20 were: *Killed* — Privates Rolin Huddleston and Franklin Russell. *Wounded* — Corporals Peter Baker, David Beaty, Asa Kite and William G. Carpenter (died September 27; married with two children); Privates Jesse M. Abbott, Elijah Gabriel, Samuel Halterman, James Miranda, Thomas Scott and John Wank; *Captured* — Sergeant Jasper N. Hall; Privates William L. Mott and Josiah McDowell (died April 16, 1864, at Danville, Va.).

6. Hall gave this man's name as Clark, but no one in the 113th Ohio by that surname was killed during the war. Company B's fatal casualties on September 20 were Privates William Lambert and John J. Smith. Two others, Sergeant Lewis H. Bell and Private Henry H. Kramer, died of their Chickamauga wounds in October 1863, while a fifth man, Samuel E. Crane, was listed missing with no further record found. [*Ohio Rosters,* vol. VIII, p. 719, 722, 724; McAdams, p. 250, 251].

7. Joshua M. Wells mustered as Company C's captain on April 19, 1863. He previously served in the company as second and first lieutenant. [J.M. Wells compiled service record, RG 94, NARA].

Nearly six months after Chickamauga, Hall's comrade Francis McAdams sent home a tribute to Wells clipped from *The Christian Banner,* reading in part: "Captain J.M. Wells was slain in the battle of the 20th September, in North Georgia. His funeral sermon was preached in Wesley (M.E.) Church, Columbus, Ohio, by his pastor, Rev. Joseph M. Trimble. In the sermon reference was made to his company bearing the flag of the regiment. When Captain Wells was shot, his orderly sergeant [William A.M. Davis] led him out of the ranks and seated him at the foot of a tree, giving him water once or twice. The Captain urged the orderly to leave him and protect the flag. On returning to look after his wounded captain, he found him looking at a daguerrotype picture of his wife and babes. This picture, with his watch and sword, he delivered to [Davis], requesting him to send them with his body to his family, telling them he died as a Christian and a soldier." [*Urbana Citizen and Gazette,* March 17, 1864].

8. On October 1, 1863, General Braxton Bragg informed Confederate

authorities in Richmond: "Unable to care properly for the enemy's wounded, I have, by special agreement, paroled and delivered to him all fit for transportation." The exchange of wounded prisoners primarily occurred the previous day. [*Official Records,* series II, vol. 6, p. 327, 335].

9. Within a week of the battle Union soldiers captured at Chickamauga began arriving by train in the Confederate capital. The *Richmond Dispatch* reported that 1,634 reached the city on September 27, "and were full of bombast. In conversation one of them informed us that he believed 'Rosecrans would get whipped this time, but he had too many pontoon bridges to cross the Tennessee and get away with.' They are the most hang-dog looking scoundrels we have ever seen, their appearance not being one-half as fine as the men of Grant's army." The following week the same newspaper told its readers that "Yankee prisoners are becoming as thick here as blackberries in harvest. There are now between six and eight thousand in the city. ... Libby Prison is crowded with Yankee officers awaiting an exchange, and the cry is 'Still they come.' Every train brings in a fresh batch of these precious Abolition jewels, to be fed and cared for at Government expense." [*Richmond Dispatch,* September 28 and October 5, 1863].

Champaign Countian Alexander H. Stanton was among the captive officers from Chickamauga. The captain of Company F, 1st Battalion, 16th U.S. Infantry, wrote to his mother a week after confinement in Libby: "We are doing as well as could be expected under the circumstances, except for clothing and blankets. ... We amuse ourselves as we can best — cards, chess, songs, and *skirmishing for greybacks.* I tried my hand at washing a shirt Saturday, but failed ignominiously. After coffee, every man strips to the buff, and the skirmishing opens vigorously. Every crack sounds the death knell of a creeper." [A.H. Stanton, October 6, 1863, in the *Urbana Citizen and Gazette,* November 6, 1863].

2

Richmond

Killing the goose that laid the sweet egg

None of us had believed that our imprisonment would last but a few days, and had expected nearly every day before leaving northern Georgia to be exchanged and returned to our commands. Upon arriving at Richmond we were marched across two long bridges which spanned the James River, below the falls, and thence down a street running parallel with the river, and thence into the famous building known as Libby.

Libby stood on the bank of the James. It was a long brick building with basement and two stories, and had probably been used as a wholesale tobacco house.[1] The long way of the building was up and down the river, or in other words, the building stood with its side to the river. On its end front was the sign "Libby & Son." Nearly four hundred of us were quartered on the lower floor of this building on our arrival, and the same evening we had issued to us a small piece of brown bread and a half pint of thin soup to each man — not half enough to satisfy our appetites. Piling ourselves upon the hard floor we rested well for the night, for the journey of several hundred miles had been one of fatigue and unrest.

Next morning the prison was visited by two Confederate officials, accompanied by half a dozen guards, and the work of robbing the prisoners of their money in a business-like manner began. We were told to surrender our money to the officers for safekeeping; that an account of it would be kept for us and the amount returned to us whenever we left the prison. We were also told that those who refused to surrender their money voluntarily would be searched, and all money thus found would not be returned. Having thirty-three dollars, I thought I would divide with them, so pulling off my boot I secreted twenty dollars therein. When my turn came to "stand and deliver," I handed over thirteen dollars and all was satisfactory. One of my fellow prisoners had four hundred dollars in gold, all of which he handed over to these robbers. Nearly every one of us had more or less money, and by the time they were through taking care of it for us they had a considerable pile of greenbacks, and they seemed thoroughly satisfied with the amount realized, for not a man was searched and the few who had the good sense to keep their money saved it all. Not a cent of this money was ever returned, nor was there any intention of returning it when it was taken. It was cowardly, heartless theft.[2]

The second day we received our rations in kind and quantity like the first, but as before the quantity was far short of our necessities, and after eating the whole quantity we were almost as hungry as before.

The next day we were marched out of Libby and put into another prison known as the "Pemberton Building." This prison stood farther east than Libby and on the opposite side of the street. It was a large three-story brick with a cellar the full size of the foundation; a brick partition divided it into two nearly equal apartments.[3] Before we were put into this prison it was already full of prisoners, but we were crowded in among the rest and now it was with great difficulty that we could find room to lie down. I, with others of my comrades, found a place on the third floor.[4]

The men on each floor drew their rations separately, and according to the number of men on each. One of our number was appointed to receive the rations for all the men on one floor, after which a sub-division was made to squads of twenty-five men, and then these twenty-five would sub-divide, giving to each man his portion with exactness, for even a crumb was a matter of contention among starving men. Our rations were cooked and prepared for us in the basement of Libby prison, and each day a certain number of men was detailed from each floor to go after them.

Our rations now consisted of a very small piece of old bacon, boiled, a half pint of thin soup made of the water in which the bacon was boiled, and a small piece of bread. This was not sufficient for one good meal a day and our hunger was never satisfied. As soon as our food, which was intended for three meals, was issued to us we ate it all in one and then hungered till the same hour the next day. I have been so hungry that when I got my soup, thickened with skippers which

Looking southeast, Richmond photographer Charles R. Rees took this image of Libby Prison possibly in August 1863. Two of the three men standing in the right foreground are reputed to be Richard Turner (middle), jailer, and Thomas P. Turner (far right), commandant.

came out of the meat in boiling, that I never pretended to separate the skippers from the soup, but greedily swallowed skippers and soup together and thought it excellent. We all did the same in this respect. Every atom of food was precious in our eyes, and being continually hungry our minds and conversation dwelt upon things we wished to eat. It appeared to us that if we could only have had enough to eat, notwithstanding our loathsome confinement, we would have been the happiest creatures alive.

Nearly every day flying reports of an exchange were circulating among the prisoners, and our hopes were alternately buoyed and depressed by these groundless rumors, originating — nobody knew where; and yet for all this they served to keep us hopeful. But as day after day passed and no exchange came, I began to despair of being speedily exchanged and began to look about and devise means and mature plans of escape. These thoughts I kept to myself, but it was several days before I struck a plan that was at all practical.

There was quite a trade, in a small way, kept up between the prisoners on the inside and the guards outside of the building. This was in violation of orders and whatever was done in this line had to be done with the utmost caution. I already had made several little trades with one of the guards, resulting in quite an intimate acquaintance, and the thought suggested itself that if I could induce this guard to sell me a Confederate uniform, I might by this means effect my escape. I approached the guard very cautiously at first, telling him that my clothes were about gone, that I did not know what I would do for more, and finally ventured to ask him how much he would charge me for a pair of gray pants and a roundabout. At first he was disinclined to sell this kind of goods, fearing that by some means it might be found out and he made to suffer. He made many excuses, saying he did not know where he could get them for me. I assured him that there would be no danger and promised him eternal secrecy. At last he agreed that for ten dollars in greenbacks he would bring me the required articles when he came on guard again that night at one o'clock. I returned to my place on the floor and waited with impatience for the intervening hours to wear away. I feared to lie down, knowing that if I fell asleep I might miss my appointment with the guard.

At last I heard the guards sing out their accustomed cry, "Twelve o'clock and all's well." One more hour to wait and then I should know of my success or failure. That hour seemed almost an age, but at length came the cry, "One o'clock and all's well." I waited a few minutes and then crept cautiously downstairs to the window near which the guard was stationed. I found him all right and told him in a low whisper to pass the clothes to me through the iron bars of the window, and I would pass the money to him in the same manner. The exchange was quickly made, and I hurried back upstairs to my sleeping companions.

After roll call next morning I put on my suit of gray and began to plan for the future. I have before stated that we procured our rations ready cooked in the basement of Libby prison across the street, and at some distance westward. When the time came to draw our rations I contrived to be detailed for that purpose, and picking up a wooden bucket I fell in line with the rest. A guard was always on duty to prevent any attempt to escape, and therefore my chances were desperate, but it could be no worse if I failed.

Generally, when the cookhouse was reached we had to wait some time before receiving our rations, and at these times the guards and prisoners were apt to be engaged in little trades of various kinds, and the guards were likely on such occasions to relax their watchfulness. It was at such a time as this that I hoped to find a chance to escape.[5]

Watching for my opportunity while the attention of the guard was drawn to some little trade, and at the same time watching for the Confederate officers, I handed my bucket to a companion with a sly nudge and look which meant silence, and slipped out of the ranks. I did not attempt to leave immediately, but stood around with some Confederate soldiers who were off duty and who were watching the prisoners out of curiosity. I asked one of the bystanders how long since these fellows had been captured, and made some further remark about thrashing the Yankees.

When the squad began drawing its rations, I sauntered slowly and carelessly up the street, passing "Castle Thunder" on my way. This building stood on the same street as Libby, two hundred yards or more farther west and not far from the river. It was a three-story brick building and was now filled with Confederate soldiers, probably deserters and those who refused to enter the rebel ranks.[6]

Being dressed in all respects as a rebel soldier, I did not attract any particular attention. As I passed on I met numbers of officers and soldiers, greeting them with the true military salute. I wandered toward the upper part of the city, intending to get out of town in the dusk of the evening. I was fearful of pursuit, for I did not know how soon I would be missed from the prison. I was risking all on one desperate chance of escape and was, therefore, in no frame of mind to enjoy the sights of that part of Richmond through which I was passing. I stopped at a small provision store kept by an Irish woman in the suburbs of the city. I bought two dollars worth of cheese and crackers, paying for the same in Confederate money, and got about enough for a full meal. I would have eaten it all on the spot, but was fearful of exciting the curiosity of the old woman by eating too greedily.

As the sun began to sink behind the western hills I walked out of the city, but it was dusk before I had passed beyond the last houses of the outskirts. Indeed, it seemed to me that the houses of the city reached a great way into the country, and every moment I feared I might meet someone who would inquire where I was from and where I was going. These were two questions which I prefered not to answer. Fortunately I saw no one who was inclined to be inquisitive.

As soon as darkness set in I left the gravel turnpike and struck out into the fields on my right. I was entirely ignorant of the country, but I knew I could not remain in or near the city long undiscovered. I must go somewhere. The night being cold and chilly, I had to keep continually on the move to keep from suffering with cold. If I had desired to start a fire I had no means to do so, therefore exercise was a necessity. I stumbled into ditches, scratched my face and hands with brambles, crossed fences and kept floundering along without any definite knowledge as to where I was going, but my plan was to pursue a northwesterly course from Richmond. I somehow thought this route would be the clearest of enemies, and that I might be fortunate enough to slip through the lines of the enemy and get into our own lines and be safe.

A short time before daylight I entered a heavy forest, and as day began to break I sat down, for by this time I was well nigh exhausted. I now ate what little food I had and waited for the sun to rise, that by that means I might be able to shape my course. I was now far out of sight of the city and sincerely hoped I might always remain so.

As the sun came up I shaped my course and moved ahead through the woods, moving slowly and cautiously; in fact, I could not have hurried if I had desired to do so. About ten o'clock I emerged from the woods onto a plantation. I could see the mansion of the planter about a mile to the right, and a little to the left of it and several hundred yards distant were the quarters of the slaves. The day was pleasant, it being the time of year when the nights are cold and the days pleasant.

Lying down behind a log I was soon sound asleep. As near as I could judge I slept till about two o'clock in the afternoon, when I was awakened by the barking of a dog. I aroused myself in some alarm, and

Another view of Libby Prison by photographer Charles R. Rees, looking east along Canal Street. A portion of the Pemberton prison building can be seen in the far left background.

looking around I saw a fierce-looking canine within a few yards of me, barking savagely as though he had found something. Rubbing my eyes, I peered about that I might be able to see the dog's master, and noticed an old gray-haired negro with an ax on his shoulder and a heavy piece of dogwood sapling under his arm. He spoke to the dog to be still and eyed me with a half-frightened look. In a moment I realized that concealment was out of the question and the best thing I could do would be to make friends with my sable visitor. The old man seemed very shy, but I spoke kindly to him, called him uncle, and told him that being exceedingly tired I had laid down to rest and had fallen asleep. He told me he was the slave of a Major Brown and that his master was in the army, as was also a younger son of his master, but that there was one of the sons at home. He asked me if I was not a soldier, too. I admitted that I was. He said he had heard that the Yankees were a very bad kind of men, and that they would coax the poor black man from home and then roast and eat him. I told him that I had no doubt but that many of them were very bad people. He told me the distance to Richmond was eleven miles and that there was a camp of troops some seven or eight miles west of us. I told him I wanted to go home to see my mother, and that if these soldiers or anyone else knew I was here they would not let me go, and that he must tell no one of having seen me. I told him then that he had better go home and that I would lie down and rest a while longer. As soon as he was out of sight I thought it unsafe to remain here longer, so I hurried away, keeping in the skirts of the woods next to the plantation on my left.

Farther on I reached a road running westward and followed it for half a mile or more, but becoming fearful of meeting Confederate soldiers or of being seen by them, I struck off into the woods on my right as the safest plan to escape observation. Traveling till near sundown, I came out into the open country again. The country through which I had traveled during the day was rough, hilly and broken, but now I found myself on the edge of what appeared to be a highly cultivated valley, with mansions and negro quarters stretching out before me as far as the eye could reach. I was now nearly exhausted from hunger and fatigue, so lying down I rested till after dark and determined on procuring something to eat, by some means, at any risk. Before night came on I had observed some negro huts in the distance, and to these I made my way, urged on by a gnawing hunger which grew keener with each passing moment.

I went first to a shanty where I could see glimmerings of light through the cracks and crevices in the wall, but upon approaching nearer the noise of laughter and confusion from within made me hesitate to enter, and I determined to call at one or more of the other shanties nearby; but at these there was no response to my knock so I was compelled to return to the first. The hungry voice within me would not be hushed, and prudence having surrendered to necessity I could only make known my desperate condition and take the consequences.

I knocked boldly at the door. The noise within at once ceased and the door was opened by a burly darkey who, upon seeing me, started back in some trepidation. At a glance I saw inside a number of negro women, young girls and children, besides four negro men, but last and worst there were four rebel soldiers in the party. Retreat was not to be thought of. I therefore walked boldly in without showing the fear that

I felt. The soldiers were considerably startled at the situation, and I think they took me to be one of their men bent on the arrest of their party. Comprehending what might be passing through their minds, I concluded the best thing to do was to play a bold hand, so I remarked to them that we had caught each other this time, but it would never do for one soldier to blow on another.

It was but a short time till things were again moving on as usual, yet I could see that I was the object of suspicion and the soldiers kept an eye on me, which showed a lack of confidence. Before my arrival one of the negroes had been playing the fiddle and the soldiers and wenches had been dancing, but my coming had dampened the enjoyment of the hour.

I asked one of the women for something to eat and showed her a bone ring which I had made while in prison, promising it to her if she would get me what I wanted to eat. She set before me a good sized piece of cornbread and a small piece of bacon, which I ate with great relish, thinking it as palatable a mess as I had ever eaten.

I intended as soon as I finished eating to step quietly out of the house and make my escape. But fate had decided otherwise, for just as I swallowed the last mouthful there came a loud knock at the door and, before anyone from within could open the door it was flung open from without, and in stepped a Confederate sergeant followed by eight soldiers with fixed bayonets. There was no chance of escape, for the only door to the room was guarded by two of the soldiers. The squad proceeded to arrest the four rebel soldiers and myself.

The negroes were kicked and cuffed shamefully, while we were threatened with severe punishment when we reached camp. The four Confederates arrested with me were known to the sergeant and his party, and I soon learned from their conversation that they had evaded duty and absented themselves from camp early in the morning. I was the extra man unaccounted for. The sergeant asked me what regiment I belonged to, and, knowing that it would be useless to tell anything but the truth, I told him I was a member of Company E, 113th O.V.I. He did not at once comprehend, and said that he knew of no such regiment about there. I did not feel inclined to enlighten him further just then, knowing that all I could say would do no good. The five of us were securely bound together, while the negroes were ordered to their respective quarters, a command they obeyed with alacrity. We were now marched off in single file in the direction of the rebel camp, which I think was about three miles distant from the place of our capture. We reached the camp about one o'clock a.m. and spent the remainder of the night in a guard house, closely guarded.

When daylight appeared I had an opportunity of looking about me and of becoming acquainted with my surroundings. The camp was situated in a grove of small timber and the troops numbered, perhaps, three regiments. I learned from my fellow prisoners that these troops were stationed here for the purpose of caring for and feeding up a lot of cavalry horses.

About seven o'clock we were furnished with a light breakfast consisting of cornbread and beef, after which we were ordered out under a guard to perform fatigue duty. I told the sergeant who had charge of the guards over us that, as I did not belong to that command, it was unjust to compel me to do such duty. I was fearful that if I waited to be found out by force of circumstances I might be taken for a spy, in which case my punishment would be death. I told the sergeant to request his captain to come and see me, as I had something of importance about which I wished to speak. The captain, a tall, well-made man with black whiskers, made his appearance and desired to know why I wanted to see him. I told the story of my escape and recapture, withholding nothing. He seemed much surprised and, promising to report my case to the colonel in command, went away. After a time two guards came and conducted me before the colonel.

There were several officers present when I was taken into the presence of the colonel, all of whom looked upon me with doubt and suspicion. The colonel questioned me very closely as to how I made my escape, where I had at first been taken, and many other questions which I do not recall, all of which I answered truthfully. After this I was returned to the guard house. I felt ill at ease for, though I had told a straight and truthful story, I could see that I was not more than half believed.

About two o'clock that afternoon a lieutenant came to the guard house and told me that they had concluded to send me to Richmond, and if I had not told the truth I would have a quick passage to the other world. This gave me relief, for at Richmond I felt confident I could establish the truthfulness of my story and my innocence in being a spy. The lieutenant and two guards then started with me to Richmond. We were all mounted on mules, I riding beside the lieutenant and the two guards in our rear. We soon became somewhat acquainted and fell into a lively conversation on the topics of the war, North and South. I told him of my services as a soldier, of being captured, and many other incidents, in all of which he seemed interested. He, in turn, recounted some of his experience in the C.S.A., and our talk became animated and pleasant, both of us wishing the war at an end so we could be at our respective homes — he in North Carolina and I in Ohio.

It began to grow dark before we reached Richmond. I was taken before the military officer in command of the city, and from there was taken to the city jail, into which I was thrust. The cell was dark, damp and loathsome. Here I spent the night, supperless. Next morning I was given a light breakfast of cornbread and soup, after which I was taken out and conducted under guard to the office of the commanding general.[7] Here I was closely questioned in the presence of several officers in regard to the plan and means of escape, and here, as before, I told a plain and truthful tale, knowing that the truth would serve me better than a lie. The general asked me if I could name anyone in the prison by whom I could establish my identity. I mentioned the names of Ed. Wright and Thomas Hinton. They were sent for and confronted me. They were much surprised at seeing me, as well as being thus called from the prison in this manner, for what purpose they knew not.

These two men were questioned separately and very closely, and their statements regarding me coincided so completely that all present were fully convinced that I had told a true story. The general lectured me soundly for my ingratitude in trying to escape from such kind friends, and said that, as a punishment, I should be sent to the dungeon for twenty-four hours.

I was accordingly taken to the city prison and thrust into an underground cell with an iron door. The cell was musty and without ventilation; the air was damp and stifling. In a corner was an old straw mattress, falling to pieces with age and filth. As soon as the guard had closed and locked the massive iron door, the intense darkness of the cell became oppressive beyond description. Not the faintest gleam of light could find its way into this abode of inky darkness. The darkest night was as brilliant sunshine compared with this dungeon. The thought of remaining here twenty-four hours was tormenting, and the fear that I might be forgotten entirely and left to die a dreadful death of hunger and thirst filled my mind with frightful fancies. None but those who have passed through a similar experience can have the least idea of the tormenting doubts which assail a person in the position I then was. Hour after hour dragged slowly away. I became feverish and desperately thirsty; my only thought now was water. If I only could have one good drink of water I thought I could endure my situation in comfort.

At length, worn out with my own thoughts, I cast myself upon that couch of filth and tried to wear away a part of my sentence in sleep. A restless sleep finally came over me, in which I dreamed of running streams of limpid water at which I was drinking, but could not slack my thirst. I awoke from my feverish sleep with a dull, heavy pain in my head and with my thirst more tormenting than before. I was now really sick. I could not tell how long I had been in this horrible place, but short as the time really was it seemed to me almost an age.

At length I heard the rattle of keys in the door. It was flung open and there stood the guard and the turnkey of the prison to conduct me beyond these hated walls. Staggering to my feet, I was soon in the upper daylight and was breathing the pure, invigorating air of heaven. It was some time before I could accustom my eyes to the glare of the sun. There was plenty of water in the prison yard, of which I drank and bathed my face, feeling much refreshed. I was then conducted by two guards to my old prison and was again locked within its walls. Those who knew me in the prison crowded around me, asking a thousand questions. I promised to tell them all at a future time, but for the present I needed rest. I went upstairs to my old place and laid down. Some of the prisoners gave me something to eat, and I fell asleep and slept till the next morning. I awoke feeling much refreshed, and though my trip to the country had not resulted as I desired, I felt that I had had some valuable experience.

Time now moved on without incident for some days. Our rations were barely sufficient to sustain life, but never enough to appease our hunger. Such of us as had money or some other means of traffic could sometimes effect a trade with the guards, and thereby procure a little extra to eat.

At length, as if by accident, we found in one part of the prison, securely locked from our reach, a quantity of wheat bran, which could be accessed by tying a tin cup to a long stick and fishing it to within our reach. By stealing this bran we were able to make mush by boiling it in our little tin buckets, but, lacking salt, the mush was very unpalatable.

I have heretofore stated that the building had a brick wall passing up through the center. There were prisoners on both sides, but they were kept separate and not allowed to communicate with one another. But by drilling small holes through the brick wall this restriction was avoided and friendly relations established.

We now ascertained that those in the other department had plenty of salt, an article of which we on our side were sadly in need. So, by increasing the size of the holes in the wall to admit a spoon we were able to transport a spoonful of salt at a time, a circumstance that added much to our comfort and traffic in salt grew active. Finally it leaked out that the salt we were buying from our fellow prisoners was found in quantity in a room of the basement on their side of the building. This induced us to prospect under our part of the building. Back next [to] the water closet was a small passage or entry. With the aid of a hatchet which had been smuggled into the prison, we tore up the floor of this entry and sent a man below to explore. He soon returned with news that the cellar under our part of the building [contained] a big strike — a regular bonanza of sugar. A door-keeper was appointed, secrecy was enjoined on all, and the utmost caution was used to prevent our good news from spreading to the authorities.

Only a few were permitted to go down for sugar at a time. The men would take off their worn and dirty drawers, tie the ankles in a knot, and watch patiently for a turn to descend into the cellar for sugar. Then, filling these lousy, filthy garments with sugar, they would return to their places. Every available article that would hold sugar was brought into use. Needles and thread were found and sacks made out of everything possible, and these filled till every man on our side of the house was plentifully supplied and had sugar to sell. On the other side they had plenty of salt, but no sugar; on our side there was a glut of sugar and a demand for salt. A brisk trade thus ensued in these two commodities and was carried on by way of the holes in the wall before mentioned. The sugar and salt added much to our comfort. The sugar served to deaden our appetites and also to sweeten our bran mush, while the salt added made it quite palatable.

The routine of prison duties was somewhat after the following order: The first thing after getting up in the morning was lousing; that is, we would pull off our clothing, give them a careful inspection and kill all the lice we could find. These were not a few. I think that on average each man would kill from three to four hundred of these parasites each day, and by the next morning there would be as many more to share the same fate.

After lousing came roll-call and after that we could steal sugar and trade with our friends for salt, or occupy our time in some other way. From one till two o'clock in the afternoon was our time to draw rations, but no more of our number were allowed to go out in a Confederate uniform as I had done. We ate our dinner about three o'clock in the afternoon, then we would sit around and talk of home, or of an exchange, or of what grand dinners we would have when we got out of prison. We usually laid down in our sleeping places as soon as dark came on, for, being without fire or lights, we kept early hours. A rule had been established among us that no one should go down for sugar except in the night, for there was danger of being discovered in the daytime.

The prison was so crowded that when the men all laid down the floor space was entirely occupied, and this led to more or less trouble between the occupants of the lower floor and those of the second and third floors. Those of the first or lower floor claimed a sort of monopoly in the sugar trade, and finally became so arrogant as to say that we from the second and third floors had no right to come down during the night to get sugar, and they would suffer it no longer.

The feeling increased from day to day and many personal encounters ensued between the monopolists on the lower floor and the occupants of the other two floors. Open rupture threatened, and my partner and I, seeing the storm coming in the distance, managed to accumulate a stock of sugar ahead, for under the heated animosity existing among the men our sugar plot would soon be made known to our captors.

About the end of the third week following the discovery of our sugar mine, the crisis was reached. The men of the two upper floors said, with emphatic profanity, that they would go down in the night and get what sugar they wanted; those of the first floor declared with equal emphasis that they would not suffer their dominion to be invaded and their dreams disturbed by intruders. So when night came on the occupants from above went below as they had promised to do, and during the whole night there was nothing but fighting and quarreling. Those from above filled their haversacks, drawers and the like with sugar, and in attempting to return to their places were set upon by the others who attempted to rob them of their sugar, or, failing in this, would rip open the sacks and other things used in carrying the sugar, and the contents were scattered on the floor.

This state of things lasted all night and resulted in the unnecessary destruction of hundreds of pounds of sugar, so that in the morning the floor where the ugly scene had occurred was covered with a coat of sticky taffy, the heat of the room having reduced the sugar to a half-melted state, so that in walking over the floor one's feet would stick at every step. Further concealment was now out of the question, and from the condition of affairs we felt satisfied we would have to face the music. We had now killed the goose that laid the sweet egg. It is unaccountably strange to see how very foolish men act at times, but it has been so and will so remain.

When the Confederate officers came in the next forenoon to call the roll, as was their custom, they at once discovered that something unusual had occurred. Their feet stuck to the floor and they soon made the discovery that we had been stealing their sugar. A rumor ran through the prison that all of us were now to be searched, and such as were found with sugar in their possession would be tied up by the thumbs as a punishment, but these reports proved to have no foundation in fact. No one was searched or punished, and those who had sugar were permitted to keep it. The Confederates estimated they lost $20,000 worth of sugar and salt, but I am inclined to think that the real loss would not reach over $6,000.

The basement of our prison was emptied of these articles the same day of the discovery, and the immediate result to us was that both rose rapidly in value, demand exceeding the supply. Sugar which could be had for nothing yesterday is today worth $2.50 per pint. Salt rose proportionately.[8]

Our rations were now cut down for a week as a punishment, and as a consequence we suffered much.

Richmond Notes

1. Libby often has been incorrectly called a tobacco warehouse. When the Civil War began it was the establishment of Luther Libby & Son, ship chandlers and grocers, located close to the James riverfront in the block bounded by Cary and Canal streets, and 20th and 21st streets. At the front the brick building was three stories high along Cary Street and four stories in the rear where the ground sloped south toward the canal. Its interior was divided into three sections by thick walls extending from basement to roof, each floor containing three rooms about 42 by 100 feet. Confiscated for Confederate government use, the Libby building received its first captives in March 1862, eventually becoming a prison primarily for Federal officers. [Lonnie R. Speer, *Portals to Hell: Military Prisons of the Civil War* (Mechanicsburg, Pa.: Stackpole Books, 1997), p. 89-91].

2. At the time, Libby's top two officials shared the last name of Turner, but apparently were not related. Captain Thomas Pratt Turner, commandant, had attended Virginia Military Institute for a year and was a strict disciplinarian. With more direct control over the prisoners as second in command, Richard R. "Dick" Turner was a former plantation overseer who, pre-war, briefly attended the U.S. Military Academy at West Point, N.Y., before being dismissed in disgrace on a forgery conviction. Prone to quick anger and physical abuse, he was described by one prisoner as "a hard and cruel reprobate." Both men were despised by those who fell under their charge for any length of time. [Speer, p. 90; Robert Knox Sneden, *Eye of the Storm: A Civil War Odyssey* (New York: The Free Press, 2000), p. 4].

Hall's account of fellow prisoners being robbed was commonly echoed by many Union soldiers entering Libby or nearby Pemberton/Crew Prison. Blame was laid squarely at the Turners' feet:

• Corporal John P. Brook, Company I, 35th Ohio — "Captured at Chickamauga, Sept. 20, 1863 ... we were placed in Pemberton Prison, opposite Libby. Here we were again searched and robbed, having twice before been subjected to the same process on the journey to Richmond. They searched even the seams of [our] clothing, and kept such articles of wearing apparel as they cared to, in some cases leaving the boys scarcely enough to cover their nakedness. [My] blanket and what little money [I] had were taken." ["His Prison Experience," *The National Tribune*, December 31, 1891].

• Corporal George S. Dunlap, Company D, 100th Pennsylvania — "Taken from Libby into a large brick building across the street from the prison, Dick Turner ordered us into single line and then told us to strip off all our

Captain Thomas P. Turner, Libby Prison commandant for much of the war.

clothes except shirt, to be searched. He said: 'If any of you Yanks has watches, jurly [jewelry] or U.S. money, I'll take it and return it to yah when yo'uns ah pahrolled.' Then we were made to strip, and Turner, with rebel soldiers behind him, went down the line and searched our clothes that were piled in front of us, and felt under our arms and around our necks to see if any valuables were concealed there. Whatever could be turned into money was taken as well as money." ["From a Prisoner's Diary," *The National Tribune,* October 15, 1903. Dunlap died in captivity at Salisbury, N.C., in January 1865].

• Corporal Benjamin Franklin Jones, Company B, 1st West Virginia Cavalry — "We were confined in the Pemberton Warehouse. ... An officer ordered a guard to search us, we not being permitted to retain on our persons any money or thing of value. The lying son of Belial then graciously informed us that the deprivation of our private property would only be temporary, that it would be restored to us when exchanged." ["Rebel Prisons," *The National Tribune,* May 19, 1904].

• Private James T. Flack, Company D, 8th Ohio Cavalry — "It was so crowded [at Libby] that some of us were taken across the street to the Pemberton Hotel, second floor. There we experienced terrible days and nights under the management of Dick Turner. We hated him worse than a viper for his tyranny." ["In Dreary Old Pemberton," *The National Tribune,* April 18, 1901].

With the war's conclusion in 1865, Thomas Turner eluded Federal capture and lived in Canada a number of years before returning to the United States and residing in Memphis, Tenn. Dick Turner was arrested and held in Libby a short time, but escaped. Re-apprehended, he was jailed in the Virginia state penitentiary until receiving a parole in June 1866. [Speer, p. 293].

3. Four stories high, the "Pemberton Building" was the former tobacco factory and warehouse of Crew & Pemberton, located just east of Libby Prison at the corner of 21st and Cary streets. It was divided in the center by a brick wall from cellar to roof. The eastern half (in which Hall was incarcerated) was called Crew Prison, or "Little Libby," while the west half was designated Pemberton Prison. Together they held some 1,600 prisoners. In 1862 the building was known as Crew's Factory Hospital and, later, General Hospital #15. [Robert W. Waitt Jr., *Confederate Military Hospitals in Richmond,* Publication 22 (Richmond: Civil War Centennial Committee, 1964); "In Richmond," *The National Tribune,* January 1, 1891].

4. Artist, mapmaker and diarist Robert K. Sneden, Company D, 40th New York, first entered Pemberton prison on November 30, 1863, selecting a place on the top floor. Ascending steep staircases to get there, he observed the lower floors' inmates were "Cavalry, infantry, and artillery, some in torn and patched uniforms, others in shirt sleeves, others half naked, all looking dirty, squalid, dejected and half starved in appearance." In the second story "were numerous tobacco presses through the centre of the room, but all the other rooms were devoid of any seat, bunk, or other accommodation. The men sat huddled on the floor in groups. Some were playing cards, others sleeping on the bare plank floor, others walking up and down listlessly, all wearing a haggard, starving, and sickly appearance. We were shouted to 'keep back from the windows,' as the Rebel guards below would shoot us if seen." [Sneden, *Eye of the Storm,* p. 166].

5. Confined nearby in Richmond's Smith prison building, Chickamauga captive Henry M. Davidson of Battery A, 1st Ohio Light Artillery, recalled a similar incident: "Two men in our prison managed to trade with the guard for suits of gray clothing, which they put on after dark one evening, and assuming an air of great importance, went to the door and announced themselves as members of the police, claiming a right to pass out. The guard allowed them to go out, and they departed on their way rejoicing. Whether they succeeded in making their escape we never knew." [H.M. Davidson, *Fourteen Months*

in Southern Prisons (Milwaukee: Daily Wisconsin Printing House, 1865), p. 58].

6. "Castle Thunder" was a prison at 18th and Cary streets comprised of three separate former commercial buildings. The largest, Gleanor's Tobacco Factory, housed Confederate deserters and political prisoners. In the other two were confined negro and female prisoners, and Federal POWs, respectively. [Speer, p. 93].

7. Hall undoubtedly referred to Brigadier General John H. Winder who, as Richmond's provost marshal, commanded the Department of Henrico. An 1820 West Point graduate, he not only was responsible for the Richmond area's prison facilities, but also for the arrest and return of Confederate deserters, and for maintenance of order in a city swelled double its normal size by the war. In November 1864 Winder assumed the duties of commissary general of prisoners east of the Mississippi River. While inspecting the prison at Florence, S.C., on February 6, 1865, he died two weeks shy of his 65th birthday of an apparent heart attack. [Ezra J. Warner, *Generals in Gray: Lives of the Confederate Commanders* (Baton Rouge: Louisiana State University Press, 1959), p. 341; Jack D. Welsh, *Medical Histories of Confederate Generals* (Kent, Ohio: Kent State University Press, 1995), p. 237].

8. A fellow Chickamauga captive belonging to the 84th Illinois who shared confinement with Hall recalled that the sugar-salt trading between the Pemberton Building's dividing wall lasted only one week, not three, before Confederate authorities learned of the pilferage. "The sugar and salt was immediately removed," the Illinoisan stated, "and it is presumed was taken to some place where it would be safe." He concurred that "Either too much noise had been made, or the owners of the sugar were suspicious that it was not safe in a cellar under so many Yankee prisoners." ["In Richmond. The Great Sugar Raid by Union Prisoners," *The National Tribune,* January 1, 1891].

Corporal John P. Brook, 35th Ohio, also weighed in: "There being about 2,000 prisoners in the building, the reader can readily imagine what a noise and confusion that many men would make in the dark, moving to and from the cellar all at one time in their mad endeavor to satisfy their craving, starving stomachs and sweeten their soured tempers. The rebel officers hearing this noise and tumult came into the prison to learn the cause, when they found sugar covering the floors. They hastened in the guard, forming the prisoners in column in the center of the floor. Guards placed, they compelled us to stand up until morning. Next day they deprived us of our scanty allowance of grub; all this as punishment for emptying nine hogsheads of sugar. I had about [a] half bushel for my share, and must say right here that the hole in the wall under the Pemberton Prison was the sweetest by far of any of the hell hole prisons in which I was confined while a prisoner of war." ["That Sugar Raid. A Chickamauga Prisoner Gives His Experience," *The National Tribune*, February 19, 1891].

3

Danville

In company which misery is said to love

Day succeeded day and one week wore into another without much note until about the first of December, when we were taken out of [Pemberton] prison and transferred to Danville, Va., about one hundred and fifty miles southwest of Richmond and about four miles from the North Carolina line. Danville was a place of 3,000 or 4,000 inhabitants, situated on the Dan River. The Dan River canal and the [Richmond & Danville] railroad leading to Richmond ran through the city. Several thousand of the prisoners at Richmond were at this time, December 1863, moved to Danville.[1]

We were quartered in large brick buildings which before the war had probably been used as tobacco warehouses. These buildings were numbered from one to six and situated in various sections of the city.[2] I was put in No. 4, a large brick building covered with a tin roof.[3] Most of these prisons were covered in the same manner. I occupied, with many others, the lower floor. On the south side of our prison was a tier of small rooms which may have been used as offices in times of peace. In one of these little rooms I and four comrades were quartered, there being two floors above us and each filled to its utmost capacity.

At the west end of this building was a stockade enclosing the end of the prison, and here was the privy and a well of water. A strong guard was placed on the outside of the prison, but there were no guards on the inside, therefore we had the freedom of the space where the well of water was. Our rations at Danville were more than they had been at Richmond and we all felt benefitted by the change, but withal we drew only enough for an ordinary meal and this was insufficient to satisfy the cravings of our appetites. The guards here were less vigilant than those who had guarded us at Richmond.

Prisoners confined as we were are ever restless and uneasy, planning some scheme to deceive their guards or plotting at some means to escape. Every day there were rumors of an exchange of prisoners, and we were always making calculations on being exchanged within a month's time. Many of the boys spent much of the time in making trinkets which they sold to the guards. These consisted of finger rings, toothpicks and breast pins, made of bone or gutta-percha. By this means something extra to eat was purchased.

After we had been at Danville a week the occupants of our room tore up the floor and found that it was about four feet above the level ground. Here we found pieces of plank, scraps of iron and tin and a few nails, which had been used in the construction of the building.

We determined to keep this matter to ourselves and the five of us at once began to plan to escape by tunneling out. The foundation of our prison was of stone and was sunk eighteen inches below the surface. Along the south side of the prison ran a wide street, and on the opposite side was a dwelling house with garden attached. We calculated that the street was sixty feet wide, and that the whole distance we would have to tunnel would be seventy-five feet. We possessed ourselves of an old hatchet and with what we had we at once began operations. Besides the hatchet we had two or three case knives and some scraps of iron. Nine o'clock in the morning was the time for roll-call, at which time we would be in our places and the planks down. We made our beds over the loose planks, and our blankets were so spread as to conceal any defects in the floor. While two of us went below to work a strict watch was kept above to prevent surprise and discovery.

Even with the utmost diligence very little progress could be made. We were compelled to dig down under and below the foundation before we could make a start at tunneling, but by the end of a week we had made a fair beginning. We concluded to lighten the labor by taking others into the secret, and accordingly four others in whom we had the utmost confidence were initiated into the plot and made acquainted with our plans and purposes. We toiled day after day nearing the accomplishment of a project which, if successful, would be life and liberty. We never went below to work till after roll-call in the morning. This we considered the safer plan, for we knew not what minute they might come in upon us.

By the end of the second week our numbers had grown to fifteen, as each of our original number had his particular friend whom he wished to favor, and every day an additional man was let into the secret. As soon as roll-call was over in the morning two of our number would go down and work for an hour, while one, pretending to be sick, would spread his blankets on that part of the floor through which we went down, thus guarding against interruption and discovery. When the hour was up two others would go below and take the places of the first two, and thus the work went on till dark, when it was suspended till the next day. We managed to make our exchanges so as not to attract the attention of the other prisoners, for to have made known our aim and object to all the prisoners would have insured its failure.

In making the tunnel one of our number would creep into the excavation, dig the dirt and fill it into a flour sack, which had come into our possession. This sack had attached to it two ropes, by means of which it was worked to and fro. When the sack was full it was pulled backward and its contents emptied out under the prison floor. It was then pulled back and refilled. In this way we worked till days grew into several weeks. We had made our way under the very feet of our guards and passed under one of the busy streets of the city. Wagons and carts and throngs of people passed over our heads, but heeding not their din we bent every effort to one coveted end.

We were rapidly approaching completion of our work and all were in the best of spirits. A few more days and we would be able to go out whenever we considered the opportunity favorable. The number interested in the tunnel had now increased to near sixty. Just how so many came to be let into the scheme I never could well tell. By a careful measurement the tunnel was one hundred and twelve feet long, and we felt confident that we were far enough into the garden to insure our escape if the nights were dark, but unluckily for us the moon just at this time was full, and we were compelled to delay our final effort to escape until the dark of the moon. We, however, made all the necessary preparations so as to be fully ready when the time should arrive. Each day some of our number would go down into the tunnel to work a little and see that all was right. All our plans were discussed and tomorrow night was fixed upon as the time for our escape.

We had barely finished laying our plans when a squad of soldiers led by a lieutenant came into the building and ordered us to pack our effects and move to the upper floors. This was as a clap of thunder in a clear sky to all who were interested in the tunnel. It dawned upon us in a moment that we had been betrayed, but by whom we could not tell.

We were all crowded up on the second and third floors, and then our captors began walking around on the first floor in order to discover any loose planks. When they reached the little room we had occupied they found what they very probably already knew to be there, namely, the loose plank which we had used as a doorway to our work. Then followed some bitter and loud profanity. They then procured a light and, going below, explored our work from end to end to their entire satisfaction.

A squad of negroes was then brought in and put to work filling up the tunnel. From a window in the upper story we watched them as they followed our subterranean channel across the street and into the garden where it terminated. We could see that we had gone a sufficient distance into the garden to have made our escape, and would certainly have done so but for the base treachery of someone. The tunnel was filled with stone and then covered with dirt. A guard was now placed on the first floor and the prisoners were all kept on the second and third floors. This made us so crowded that it was with great difficulty we found space to lie down.

No more of us were allowed to remain on the first floor, but ten were permitted to go down at a time, under guard, to get water and for other necessary purposes, and when these ten returned another ten were allowed to go in the same manner, and this going by tens was kept up day and night, the prisoners being required to fall in line and await their turns. In addition to the guard kept on the first floor there was also one stationed in the little backyard where the well of water was situated. Besides these, there was a strong guard at regular intervals around the prison building. Escape seemed next to, if not absolutely impossible, but prisoners confined as we were are ever restless and ready at all times to resort to desperate means to gain their freedom.

Not long after the discovery of our tunnel ten prisoners went below at night in the usual manner to procure water. When they reached the backyard which I have before described, one of them approached the guard and asked him if he wanted to trade for a gutta-percha finger ring. (The guards were always on the trade when they had the oppor-

An 1865 lithograph showing four of Danville, Virginia's six prison buildings. The view was based on a drawing by Corporal Joseph M. Thurston of Company F, 90th Ohio, who like Sergeant Hall was captured at Chickamauga.

tunity). The guard replied that he did not know and wanted to see the ring. While the guard was looking at it and dickering about the price, a prisoner approached him from behind and dealt him a heavy blow on the head, felling him to the ground. Another prisoner had stationed himself near a small gate which formerly had been used as a passageway in and out, but which of late had been securely barred by heavy oak planks nailed crosswise. As soon as the guard was knocked down the prisoner at the gate began to knock off these planks, using for the purpose an old ax with which he had provided himself before coming downstairs.

The result was that ten made their escape through the guards on the outside of the prison. The guard who was knocked down began screaming as if suffering from a horrible nightmare, and the guard on the lower floor of the prison was so shocked with fear that more than fifty of us prisoners, rushing downstairs, passed by him without opposition. We surmised that a break for liberty was being made and we all rushed for the place of exit. But the alarm had been sounded to guards on the outside, and on our reaching the gate we were met by a company of Confederate soldiers with fixed bayonets who made us hurry back upstairs about as fast as we had come down. Nine of the ten men who made their escape were captured and returned to prison. Of the tenth I never learned of his recapture or successful escape.

Soon after this last occurrence I was taken sick with typhoid fever and laid in my place on the floor suffering intensely. The hum of conversation and other necessary noises of the prison greatly aggravated my suffering, and as I was without medical attention my condition became alarming. I was at length moved out of the prison and placed in a hospital nearly a mile from the town.[4] Here I enjoyed the comforts of a clean bed and pure air, and besides was given some attention by the doctors. I remained very low for about three weeks — so low that a part of the time I was unconscious of what was passing around me. Finally, my strong constitution enabled me to weather the storm and I was in a fair way of recovering my accustomed good health. My appetite returned and I was able to be up a part of each day and walk about the ward.[5]

I began to congratulate myself on a rapid recovery, but one evening about a week after I commenced moving about I felt so ill of a sudden that I was scarcely able to reach my bed, and my fever seemed to have returned with all its original malignity. I thought that by some means I had taken a relapse and I began to think I would soon be paroled into the next world.

After taking my bed I became violently delirious, and I have a vivid recollection of that terrible night of scorching fever. I imagined myself in a hundred different fearful positions. At one time I seemed to be cut up into numerous pieces, placed in a wheel and whirled round with lightning velocity, then I would suffer from some other hallucination. The next morning my fever abated somewhat and I felt better. When the doctor made his customary morning rounds he looked at me a moment and then directed the nurses to carry me out of the ward, telling me at the same time that I had the small-pox and that it would not do for me to stay there.

A little while before this the small-pox had broken out among the prisoners at Danville, and I had in some manner been exposed to it. The nurses carried me to an old outbuilding which had the siding partly knocked off it, and which was situated at some distance from the rest of the buildings. Here already were a dozen or more prisoners with the same disease, furnishing the company which misery is said to love. I now realized that my situation was a desperate one and I nerved myself to endure and suffer much.

On the following day several other small-pox patients were brought in, and at the end of the third day our number had increased to forty, thus crowding the old building to its utmost capacity and creating a picture of sickness and suffering that would appall the stoutest heart. We were crowded and piled together in a manner that would have been very uncomfortable to men in health.

Some of our number had the disease in its most malignant form; most of these died. Others were afflicted in a milder form and a majority of these soon recovered. All night long was heard the moaning of the sick and the ravings of the delirious. Much less attention was paid us than our suffering condition demanded. We were left to get well or die, as the case might be, and those who recovered did not owe their recovery to careful nursing.

Sometimes a patient would become delirious, get out of bed and walk out into the cold and snow barefoot, and would have to be brought back. Such cases as this invariably died. Those who died during the night were suffered to remain with us till morning and then carried out for burial. Our dead numbered three, sometimes four each night. It was indeed a charnel-house of death and misery; life and death struggled for the mastery, and death usually won. Those who escaped death and recovered did so by passing through the most trying scenes and by being blessed with constitutional vigor that defied the ravages of disease. Fortunately for myself, I had the disease in its mildest form and on that account weathered through. The small-pox at length spread to the main prison buildings in town, and the pest-houses being already full to overflowing, many suffered and died of the disease without being removed from the prisons, and the cases of small-pox became so general as to excite very little attention.[6]

After about four weeks I had so far recovered as to be able to go about, and my appetite was so improved that I could have eaten much more than I did if I could have had it. Sometimes I was fortunate enough to have given me the rations of some other unfortunate comrade who was too sick to eat, and in this manner I sometimes met the demands of my appetite. I have no means of knowing the number of deaths from this disease, but there were a great many. Having no means of guarding against the contagion and being crowded closely together in unventilated rooms teeming with stench, dirt and filth, our condition invited the disease, and in the majority of cases it could not be otherwise than fatal.

After a time I was returned to the hospital from which I was taken when attacked with the small-pox. Here I was allowed two light meals a day, consisting of bread and soup, but in no case was this sufficient to satisfy my hunger.

Some days later I was placed in another hospital nearer town and was appointed ward-master in the same.[7] This hospital had two wards below and two above, and all were filled with sick. The worst cases were in the ward to which I was assigned, and my duties were such that I had four assistants under me. The number of patients under my charge was usually sixty and the deaths were often six a day. As soon as one died and was carried away his place was supplied with another patient.

Over our hospital building, as a sort of general superintendent, was a Confederate officer named Daffan. This Daffan passed through the wards each day gathering up the property of the dead men, saying that he had to account to our government for all the property of the dead. A short time previous to this the federal government had supplied the prisoners with many articles of clothing, besides blankets and other articles of comfort, and many of us had good pants, shoes, blouses and shirts. Whenever one of the men died, Daffan would come around inquiring for the "effects" of the deceased, as he called them, and everything of value was gathered together and handed over to old Daffan. He was particular to impress on our minds that he had to account to our government for all these things. We knew all the time that he was lying to us, but it would not help the matter to tell him of it. Several times we put the good clothing on the bodies of the dead and they were buried with these on. This very much displeased Daffan, who said it was all a needless waste, and threatened me that if I allowed the like to occur again he would have me returned to prison. The old fiend said that a man was just as well off by being buried in his old clothes, and no better off for being buried in his best, and that our federal authorities would be greatly displeased when they learned of this waste. I regarded this as a piece of cool impudence on the part of Daffan, to think that

I would believe a story so full of deceit and falsehood, but I kept from expressing what I thought, for I knew that anything I might say would do no good and would only aggravate him to inflict some indignity upon me.

I had now recovered my accustomed health and by a better supply of food was improving daily, having the opportunity of keeping myself more clean than I could in the prison. Daffan made his usual rounds, demanding of the attendants the effects of the dead.

Of the number of dangerously sick was a Dutchman who occupied a cot in one of the tiers near the center of the ward. Across the aisle from him lay a patient who had on a pair of good shoes, articles of which the Dutchman was entirely destitute. When this man died the Dutchman insisted so hard that I should let him have the shoes that I told him I was liable to get into trouble if I let him have them, but if he would get up and get them himself I would pretend that I knew nothing of it, and I would offer no objections. This he did, and the coveted shoes were placed under his own bunk. When Daffan came in to take possession of the dead man's effects he overlooked the shoes, and the Dutchman remained in peaceable possession of them.

It was reported and generally believed in the hospital that this Dutchman had four or five hundred dollars in greenbacks stowed away somewhere about his person, and Daffan had said to one of the nurses that the old man had better give that money over to him for safekeeping till he got well.

On the night of the third day after the shoes had changed owners, while one of the nurses and I were seated quietly by the stove, we heard the labored breathing of the Dutchman, and taking a light we went to his bed and found that he was indeed dying. He survived but a few minutes after we first heard his heavy breathing. Our custom was that when a patient died the body was placed in a suitable position, and if at night the remains were left on the cot till morning. It was a singular fact that nearly three-fourths of the deaths occurred in the night, but why this was so I could never determine.

At the time of this Dutchman's death only myself and one attendant were up, and we performed the necessary work of preparing the body for burial on the following morning. The nurse and I talked over the matter of the wealth of the deceased, and we both expressed a desire to know the truth of the report of his keeping a large amount of money about him. We concluded that if we found it we could use it to as good advantage as Daffan could, and we made diligent search in the bed and clothing of the dead man, hoping to gain possession of the reputed wealth and disappoint Daffan by keeping it ourselves. Our search was rewarded by finding only a few dollars of Confederate money and some trinkets of very little value. We were now satisfied that the report about his having a great quantity of greenbacks was a hoax, and we confessed ourselves disappointed.

The next morning the body was removed in the customary manner by placing it in the dead-house. Daffan came into the hospital later in the morning and, learning of the Dutchman's death, made inquiry for his effects. I gave him all that had been found and noticed Daffan appeared much disappointed. He asked if we did not find a quantity of greenbacks and we assured him that nothing of the kind had rewarded our search. He remarked that it was very strange indeed, and we read in his looks that he suspicioned me of having the dead man's money, but he went out of the ward and did not return immediately. In a short time, however, he came back accompanied by four soldiers with fixed bayonets and, after telling me that I was suspected of having the dead man's cash, he ordered them to search me thoroughly. They proceeded to a careful inspection of every possible and impossible place about my person where money could or could not be concealed; they ripped open the collar of my overcoat, but the imaginary lost treasure was nowhere to be found. Then they turned their attention to my mattress and pillow, and straw after straw of both these articles was made to undergo careful scrutiny. Other parts of the ward also were carefully searched, but nothing was found for the reason that there was nothing to find.

Notwithstanding the fact that I had been vindicated by the result of this search, I was from this time on a marked man and under the ban of suspicion. I was immediately deprived of my position as ward-master and was made to perform duties of the most menial kind, and every effort was put forth to inflict upon me some type of humiliation and insult. After a few days I was sent back to my old prison in town. I had been at the hospital some three months, and in that time had suffered from typhoid fever and small-pox, but had recovered from both, so that now I was much improved in my general health, and was looking and feeling better than at any time since the beginning of my imprisonment. Spring was now close at hand, for as near as I can remember it was about the middle of March or perhaps a little later.

Many changes had taken place in the prison during my absence; many had sickened and died. Some of my special friends had been carried out to the hospital, and of the many but a few had returned. From the hospital they had been carried to the dead-house, and from there to the dwelling place of the martyred dead to join the unreturning throng.

The small-pox continued to prevail in the prison, but it had become much milder in its character and was now much less dreaded than formerly. Our captors still maintained a strong guard on the lower floor and in the backyard, and but three persons were permitted to go downstairs and out to the well at a time. So many had died in the three months of my absence that the prison was much less crowded than when I left. The chances for escape by the back gate or by tunneling were now hopeless, and I soon settled down in my old place, made some new acquaintances in place of many of the old ones who had died, and resigned myself to whatever awaited me.

Our rations had become extremely light — barely enough to keep us ravenously hungry all the time — and kept our minds and conversation dwelling on imaginary feasts which we were to enjoy in the future.

In the beginning of our imprisonment we had allowed ourselves to hope for a speedy exchange; but now that weeks were lengthened into months hope was succeeded by despair, and we no longer allowed ourselves to encourage hope of release in this way. The only thing left for us to do to obtain freedom from our prison life was to plan and perfect an escape. Being carefully guarded day and night this was no easy task, and required strategy and daring of a superior kind.

Adjoining our prison was another building, the roof of which covered about one-third of the window on the north side of our building, and this seemed to offer a possible chance of escape. If we could manage to saw off the bars which covered this window, remove the glass and crawl out upon the roof of the addition, there was a chance of jumping to the ground, a distance of ten or fifteen feet from the eaves. By choosing a dark night and making the effort so suddenly as to surprise the guards, it was thought to be barely practicable, but our situation was so gloomy that our desperation nerved us for the trial. Consulting among ourselves, we concluded that if a number should undertake it at a time, crawl out on the roof, jump off and attempt to escape by running, there was a possibility of some of our number escaping. The work of sawing off the bars had to be done on the same night of our attempted escape, for to remove the bars and let the work remain to be completed at a future time would have been fatal to the plot. The undertaking required the strictest secrecy. The first steps were taken by making a number of case knives into saws.

The leader in this matter was a shrewd Irishman named John Foy. Ed. Mitchell, another Irishman, Tom Hinton, my partner, and myself were the originators and prime movers in the work.[8] One part of our plan was to keep the scheme to ourselves until the arrival of the night when it was to be carried out, and then make it generally known and induce as many to join us as dared to do so, thus increasing our individual chances of escape. We determined to wait for a dark, rainy night, for at such a time our guards were less vigilant than on other occasions.

It was not long till a favorable night arrived, and we set to work with a will to execute what we had been so long and hopefully planning. As soon as we began sawing at the window bars it became known in the prison that an attempt to escape was to be made that night, and about fifty or sixty of the prisoners expressed their intention of making the effort along with us.

We sawed away at the bars by turns until about half past eleven o'clock at night, when we succeeded in removing one bar, making an opening sufficiently large for a man to squeeze through, and nothing was now left but to determine who should follow. By this time more than one-half the number who had been so ready to escape with us had experienced a change of heart, and had gone off and laid down, preferring to bear their present terrible misfortunes rather than attempt what seemed a barely possible chance of bettering their condition. To us who had originated the plan, this determination on the part of our comrades had no effect tending to change our purpose, for we had reckoned the cost and weighed the risks before we began.

The rain which had been falling during the early part of the night now ceased, and glimpses of bright sky could be seen here and there through the clouds. It appeared to us that it was a remarkably light night, although cloudy with no moon at all. Now that the night began to grow lighter, thus decreasing our chances of escaping unobserved by the guards, we began to debate whether to go on with our half-executed project or to abandon it altogether. To us prisoners, situated in a dark room and full of fear and anxiety, every outside object seemed magnified; indeed, I sometimes seemed to think that the light itself was magnified. Our numbers, too, were fast dwindling, and out of the many who were so ready to go at the beginning, scarcely a dozen remained firm to their original intention.

Counseling over the matter we tarried till half past twelve or one o'clock. If we failed to go now our work would be discovered in the morning and we would, in all probability, be made to suffer for what we already had done. At last Foy, who was standing nearest the window, turned to the rest of us and said in a whisper that if any of us would follow, he would creep out. We told him to go on and we would be with him.

He crept out, Mitchell followed, then Hinton, and then myself. Our plan was to reach the roof and all remain quietly on the same until all who made the attempt were ready, then to drop to the ground and each for himself, escape as best he could. I handed my haversack to the man who was to follow me; it contained a piece of cornbread which was to be my subsistence until fortune supplied something more. In creeping out I fancied I made much more noise than any of those who preceded me, and on reaching the roof I could see the dim outlines of my three adventurous companions who had crept out in advance of me, each crouching closely to the roof to avoid being observed by the guards who were pacing to and fro in the darkness, but a few feet below.

I turned around in a half-straightened position to reach for my haversack, and in doing so I made a cracking noise on the roof which alarmed my comrades, and they commenced jumping from the building to the ground below. In a moment the guards began firing and shouting the alarm at the top of their voices, and the utmost excitement prevailed both inside and outside of the prison. The shouts of the guards and the reports of their guns were anything but music to our ears. I had not yet jumped. If it had been possible I should have returned to the prison in the same manner I had escaped, but in doing so I would be compelled to crawl back slowly and the guards, being now fully aware of our place of escape, would have riddled me with musket shots.

A train of thought ran through my mind with lightning rapidity, and I saw that my safest plan of action was to jump to the ground, imitating the example of my comrades and share their fate. I accordingly leaped off the building into the darkness below, striking on my feet and falling heavily forward on to my knees and hands. I jumped right over the heads of three of the guards and so close to them that they could have touched me with their guns. Each of the three fired at me, but strange to say none of the shots took effect; the darkness of the night and the confusion of the moment rendered their aim unsteady, the balls overshooting me. I was blinded by the flash of their pieces and somewhat shocked by striking the ground, but before they could lay hold of me I sprang forward and made my escape. They probably were of the opinion that their shots had killed me, and they being in no haste to secure a dead man, I had the better chance of getting away.

In my haste and fright I ran across the street and collided with a plank fence, for though I knew the fence to be there I was too much excited to remember it at that moment. The force with which I struck the fence knocked me down and I was for some minutes too much stunned to proceed. All was excitement and confusion in and about the prison. I was now on the opposite side of the street from the prison and knew nothing of the fate of my comrades. As soon as I was somewhat recovered I commenced crawling along the fence in order to get away from the immediate vicinity.

I continued to crawl until I came to a corner of the fence opposite Prison No. 3, when I was able to turn to the left and to move on, still crawling and hugging the ground with the utmost caution to prevent the guards from No. 3 seeing me. Having passed No. 3, I raised to a half-standing position and by so doing attracted the attention of the guards of No. 4. These called out, "Here goes one of them," and began firing at me. I sprang into the street and ran as fast as I could. The alarm brought nearly twenty guards in pursuit of me, and with yelling, shooting and running the chase soon became more interesting than agreeable to me.

I would trip and fall on my knees, then gathering myself up again and hurry on, realizing each moment that my pursuers were gaining on me and the shots from their guns whistled uncomfortably close by. Just as I was at the point of giving up I came to a ditch, over which was a short bridge, under which I took refuge, sinking myself as far as possible into the mud and water with which it was filled. My pursuers, owing to the darkness, failed to notice my jumping into the ditch and so proceeded further on, crossing the bridge under which lay their victim, or jumping the ditch above and below. After they had passed I sunk myself deeper into the mud and rested there for some time; meanwhile the guards, having lost track of their game, returned cursing, swearing and wondering at what had become of me.

After all was quiet I commenced crawling down the ditch, fearing all the time that if I left it I would be discovered and retaken. I proceeded in this way till I reached the mouth of the ditch where it emptied into the canal. The canal and river being on one side and the town on the other made my progress somewhat uncertain. I could not cross the river and to pass through the city, even at night, would be attended with great danger. I at length moved on, creeping as I went with the canal and river on my right and the town on my left.

Finally I came to a house, back of which was a high plank fence enclosing a garden. This fence ran so near the canal that I could not go back of it, and if I went in front I would strike the street and be in danger of being seen. The fence was too high for me to climb and under the circumstances I hesitated what to do. I halted for a time, debating with myself how to proceed.

While thus considering, I saw at a short distance a creeping form approaching me, which at first I feared might be one of the pursuing guards, but my second thought led me to hope it might be one of my comrades, so acting upon this conclusion I crept toward it. It proved to be my dear friend Hinton, and though we met under the darkest circumstances the meeting was a joyous one for both.

We congratulated each other on our fortunate meeting and for a time consulted as to future plans. Hinton could relate very little of the fate of Foy and Mitchell, but said that when the first shots were fired at the prison he heard someone say he was shot, but could not tell who it was. Hinton's wrist was badly sprained and swollen, and was paining him very much; this was the result of his jump from the prison roof. We determined to cross the street in our front and pass up another one leading to the suburbs in a western direction, and finally out of town.

The canal and river shut off our escape in that direction and we felt certain that to remain here till daylight would result in our recapture. We therefore walked out across the street in our front and passed up another one to the outer edge of the town without meeting or seeing a single person, and without being seen. Once or twice we were bayed at by some dogs that ought to have been asleep at this untimely hour. Reaching a pike entering town from the west, we struck out in a brisk walk and soon left the town with its hated prisons far behind us. We congratulated ourselves anew, and began to think ourselves real heroes.

We soon concluded that it was very risky to travel on the pike and we took to the fields on our left, leaving the river and canal on the right. The rain of the past few days had saturated the earth and the fields through which we made our way were miry in the extreme, making our progress slow and difficult. The fields were enclosed with high picket fences, similar to those bound around gardens in the North, and we were often compelled to creep through holes in the fence. Sometimes we tore off the pickets in order to proceed in a direct course. Being very much exhausted with the labors and excitement of the early part of the night, and having but little vigor and strength in the beginning, we found ourselves almost completely worn out. Although we desired to go as far before daylight as possible, we were at length forced to halt and rest.

The great difficulty of traveling through the fields and the greater ease of traveling on the pike eventually induced us to return to the pike, intending when daylight came to abandon the road, return to the fields and conceal ourselves. We had reached the pike and were moving along finely when all at once several gruff voices ordered us to halt. At the same time the clicking noise which accompanies the cocking of muskets gave emphasis to the command. Our strength was so near exhausted that we could barely walk. Therefore, escape by flight was not to be considered.

Blinded by the darkness, we had run into a squad of the enemy's pickets that was guarding a ferry on the river, and had approached to within a few feet of them before we were halted. We had no knowledge of a ferry at this place and were not suspecting the presence of the enemy's pickets. I think the guards were placed here more to intercept rebel deserters than to recapture escaping prisoners. These guards already had been notified of the escape of prisoners from the town and were on the lookout for us. Our captors taunted us on the failure of our effort to escape, and said, "You-uns might have known you could not get away from we-uns." We bore their taunts with meek submission, not deigning a reply.

A sergeant and four men were detailed to take us back to town. On the way I suffered much from thirst and asked the guards to allow me to lie down at a pool and drink. This they refused to do, fearing perhaps that in some way I might effect an escape again. It was broad daylight when we reached town. I was covered with mud from head to foot, my hair was matted with mud and dirt, I had lost my hat and altogether presented a sorrowful sight.

One Moffitt [Mason Morfit], a major in rank, commanded at Danville at this time, and to his headquarters we were taken.[9] The major had not yet gotten out of bed, but presently he made his appearance, looking sour and cross. He was a small man, having dark, penetrating eyes and an ugly Roman nose, and was altogether such a man as a prisoner would prefer not to meet before breakfast. He eyed us with a look that threatened annihilation and then said viciously, "I will make you fellows pay for causing us all this trouble."

The sergeant was then ordered to take us up to the prison and leave us on the lower floor until further orders. The sergeant obeyed, placing us on one side of the building and under the care of a lank, long-haired son of chivalry as guard, telling the guard that we were a desperate couple and to shoot us upon the slightest effort to escape. The guard placed himself in a valiant attitude and, pointing a long, dirty finger at us, said, "Now, Yank, you attempt to move and I will put a ball through you in a moment." We assured him that we knew escape was impossible, and therefore we should not attempt it. As soon as the sergeant had gone out our guard told us to lie down and rest if we wished; that he was just doing that bully-talking in the sergeant's presence for effect, and that he had no desire or intention to harm us.

The other prisoners were coming downstairs and returning continually on their trips for water, and all availed themselves of getting to see us, as we were objects of curiosity. The guard was instructed to allow no conversation between us and the other prisoners, though we prevailed on him to let our friends from upstairs bring us something to eat. They brought us some cornbread and sassafras tea, which was a real treat to us.

Upon inquiry we learned that our comrade Mitchell, who had attempted to escape with us the preceding night, had been shot through the left breast and was now lying upstairs alive, but not expected to recover. And in an hour after we were placed under guard in the prison Foy was brought in. He had a badly sprained ankle, the result of jumping from the building. He had succeeded in getting out of town, but found himself unable to travel. After daylight a negro came across him and Foy offered the negro ten dollars if he would feed and care for him until he would be able to travel. This the negro, through fear, refused to do, but went away and informed the Confederates where he was to be found. He was accordingly captured and brought in.

They now had all four of us, and we were in a sorry plight. Hinton had a sprained wrist, Foy a sprained ankle and Mitchell was fatally shot. I had escaped serious injury, but was very stiff and bruised in jumping from the roof to the ground.

Soon after Foy was brought in the three of us were taken into the middle of the street and bucked. This punishment was inflicted upon us in plain view of the men in both Prison No. 4 and No. 3. We were placed about midway between the two buildings, the object being to make the lesson an impressive one to the other prisoners and to humiliate us at the same time.

Old soldiers know what bucking means, but the ordinary reader needs some explanation. The hands are tied together in front, then the body is bent down and the knees bent up, while the arms pass down the outside of the knees. Then a stick is thrust under the knees and over the arms, and the work is done. When a man is bucked he is utterly helpless, and the position of the body is so cramped that the situation becomes unendurably painful. In this case the cords were tied very tight on our wrists, which greatly increased our suffering, and our hands and arms were soon very much swollen. I began to study up a plan of relief from my painful position, and thought of a hundred different ways but all seemed useless.

After suffering for two hours my limbs became numb with the pain

I was enduring. All at once a thought struck me which seemed to be the thing, and I concluded to try it. Whirling myself on to my back I commenced struggling with a *fit*. I had seen many persons in fits and I hoped to accomplish something by a close imitation of the genuine. I rolled up my eyes with a stony, vacant stare, grated my teeth, worked the spittle into a froth and forced it into the corners of my mouth, and so contorted my limbs and body as to closely resemble the symptoms of a fit. This attracted the attention of the guards at once, and one of them inquired of the others what it meant. The reply was that he did not know, but he believed the fellow was in a fit. Another suggested that they ought to untie me, for in that condition he feared I would soon die.

The result was as I had planned it should be; they came to me, cut the cords that bound me and then left me to "come to" at my leisure. I found it more difficult to recover from than to simulate the fit, but I managed to do so with fair success. After rolling upon the ground for a short time in apparent unconsciousness, I raised myself to a sitting posture and looked around me in a half idiotic manner, pretending not to understand what had happened.

At length I sat up and seemed to be recovering consciousness. My companions and the guards were completely taken in by my acting and as I began to recover they approached and plied me with numerous questions, all of which I answered in a foolish manner. A guard asked me if I was subject to these spells. I answered that I guessed I was, but that I did not know. Finally the lieutenant turned to Foy and asked him if I was subject to fits. Foy replied promptly that I was.

This settled the matter for the time and the lieutenant walked away. I now felt that I had accomplished a point and made a good thing of it by my little acting job, and began to congratulate myself on its success. By signs I communicated to Foy that it was all "put on," and that it was done for a purpose. I must have been detected in this, for the lieutenant, who had been watching me closely, approached me and said, "Young man, I guess you have been playing 'possum' on us." He then ordered the guards to tie me up again. To this I did not protest, for, having been untied for more than an hour I felt that it was quite an item in my favor.

We were kept tied till late in the afternoon and then cut loose and left for a time to ourselves till we were sufficiently recovered to walk, when we were taken back to our former places in the prison. We were cautioned not to repeat our efforts to escape, and were threatened with worse punishment in case we did. Our hands and wrists were swollen, our legs and bodies sore from the effects of our long and painful punishment, and it required all our efforts to walk.

Our daring comrade, Mitchell, died from the effects of his wound on the third day after being brought in.

Viewing this effort to escape, after all the circumstances are made plain, I am of the opinion that our guards were made acquainted with our plans and that these were communicated to them by spies in the prison, who were sharing imprisonment for the only purpose of keeping watch over our conduct and of reporting to the rebels any attempt on our part to escape. These represented themselves to us as captives from the Union army. If our captors had not been apprised of our intentions to escape, there would not have been so many at that particular point where we hoped to find the fewest, and these would not have been prepared to shoot with such promptness as they did when we commenced jumping from the building. But for this espionage on the part of our enemies we would have certainly taken them by surprise and rendered our escape possible. I am now fully convinced that after our first effort to escape that spies were kept in our prison day and night, and that our sayings and doings were reported to the authorities.

From this time until our removal there was not the slightest chance to escape. Every avenue leading to liberty was carefully watched and strongly guarded.

Our rations all this time were hardly enough to sustain us from one day till the next, and but for the hopes of liberation and return to home, friends and plenty our desperate circumstances would have driven us mad.

All the endearments of home, the companionship of friends, the social and family ties, and the many blessings from which we seemed forever separated were the topics of our conversation by day and the subject of our dreams at night.

Danville Notes

1. To alleviate overcrowding in Richmond's prisons and the inherent problems of supply and security, General Robert E. Lee on October 28, 1863, had suggested to Confederate Secretary of War James A. Seddon that Danville might be a suitable place for prisoner relocation. There, Lee stated, "wood is cheap and provisions are in abundance, [and] there is little danger of any raid or attack from the enemy. ..." Seddon concurred, replying to Lee three days later that "Arrangements are being made to send a considerable portion [of Union prisoners held in Richmond] to Danville." Between November 14 and 17 the first 4,000 of Richmond's 13,000 POWs arrived at Danville's new facilities. [*Official Records,* series II, vol. 6, p. 438-439, 455-456; Speer, p. 126; Davidson, p. 67].

2. Most of the six buildings commandeered for prison use were located in Danville's central business district, and previously had been tobacco or cotton warehouses. Prisoner-of-war memoranda in Hall's compiled service record give December 12, 1863, as the date he was sent to Danville.

3. Prisons No. 1 through 4 were located near the intersection of Spring and Union streets. Hall's building, No. 4, was a warehouse owned by John W. and C.G. Holland, the former being president of Danville's common council. [Speer, p. 127; *Official Records,* series II, vol. 6, p. 889].

4. Hall's compiled service record indicates he was admitted to the hospital on December 24, 1863. Danville's smallpox hospital was located a mile west of town. With construction begun as early as December 17, 1863, three buildings comprised the wards where patients received treatment. Adjoining were a cookhouse, steward's office and a dead-house, all built with undressed pine lumber. A nearby spring provided fresh water. [F. Lawrence McFall Jr., *Danville in the Civil War* (Lynchburg, Va.: H.E. Howard, Inc., 2001), p. 56, 59].

5. Commenting on hospitalization in Confederate prisons, Asa B. Isham, a 7th Michigan Cavalry lieutenant who spent seven months in captivity, declared that "It may be said of the prison hospitals at Richmond and Danville that, by comparison with other such places in the Confederacy, they were entitled to be considered luxurious sick quarters. Not that any delights were ever experienced by the sick there which the memory would fondly linger over, but they were provided with bunks and beds, enough straw, old blankets, and quilts to afford them warmth, together with enough wheat bread, and soup hash, made up of meat and potatoes, to support life in a well man, however much unsuited such a diet might be to the wants of the sick." [A.B. Isham, "Care of Prisoners of War, North and South," *Sketches of War History 1861-*

1865, vol. II (Cincinnati: Robert Clarke & Co., 1888), p. 221].

6. The smallpox outbreak *was* of great concern to many Danville residents, including the town's mayor, common council and board of health. A January 27, 1864, petition signed by more than 50 citizens claimed "The stench arising from the C.S. prisons in this place, and in which there are some 4,000 Yankee prisoners confined, many of them suffering from smallpox and other virulent diseases, is so extremely offensive to the neighborhood in which we respectively reside as not only to subject us and our families to the greatest degree of annoyance, but, as we are informed by our physicians, to render it almost certain that the most fearful and fatal diseases must soon be brought upon us." Danville mayor Thomas P. Atkinson urged Secretary of War Seddon in a letter the following day "for the removal of the Yankee prisoners located among us to some other place, or at least outside the limits of the corporation of Danville." He complained the "stench from the hospitals even now (in winter) is almost insupportable," and that effluvia emanating from them "runs down in small sluggish branches that run nearly through the breadth of the town, and it is permitted to remain until a rain partially removes it, the most of it finding a permanent lodgment in the drains. The town has no water-works to cleanse its streets." [*Official Records,* series II, vol. 6, p. 888-889, 890]. To the entreaties of Danville's civic leaders there is no record of any War Department response.

7. Hall likely was referring to the large hospital complex, completed in late February 1864, near Danville's Lynn Street on the northeast slope of "Monument Hill." Hospital Steward Solon Hyde of the 17th Ohio Infantry, likewise captured at Chickamauga and assigned to one of the new wards, recalled that each building of this hospital "was fifty by two hundred feet, boxed with rough lumber, and two stories high. A hall above and below divided them into four wards, each containing sixty bunks, and each bunk supplied with a straw bed, straw pillow, and sufficient covering of quilts to make the men comfortable. ... Without exception they were the best arranged and most commodious hospital buildings I saw in the South." [McFall, p. 59-60; Solon Hyde, *A Captive of War,* edited by Neil Thompson (Shippensburg, Pa.: Burd Street Press, 1996), p. 50-51].

8. Captured at Chickamauga, Private John Foy belonged to Company A, 16th U.S. Infantry. The exact identities of the other two men have not been positively determined.

9. Major Mason Morfit, former prison quartermaster in Richmond and railroad transportation agent, commanded Danville's prison guard forces from December 23, 1863, until October 12, 1864, when he was assigned as prison

quartermaster at Salisbury, N.C. [Speer, p. 127; *Official Records,* series II, vol. 7, p. 974].

Although one Pennsylvania prisoner thought Morfit "treated us as kindly as it was possible for anyone to do under the circumstances," a majority of Danville's inmates expressed contempt toward him. Commented Ohioan Henry Davidson: "If but one-half of the enormities practiced upon help-less prisoners, under his orders, could be told with decency, the vile odors of those Danville stables, where we were kept, would be fragrance to the stench of his memory." [McFall, p. 58; James I. Robertson Jr., "Houses of Horror: Danville's Civil War Prisons," *The Virginia Magazine of History and Biography,* vol. 69, no. 3, July 1961, p. 339].

4

Andersonville

Desperate, delirious defiance toward the grim monster

About the first of April 1864 rumors circulated through the prison to the effect that we were soon to be sent to some other point. We regarded this as good news, for it seemed to us that a change might result in improving our condition, while it seemed impossible that it could make it worse.

We grew to hate the name of Danville and longed for the day when we could forever shake its dust from our feet and start for some other place, we cared not where. That long-looked-for day came at last.

About the first of May the first load of prisoners was taken from Danville and those left behind were ignorant of their destination, but learned after a short time that they had been sent to a prison somewhere in Georgia.[1] A week later the occupants of our prison building received orders to leave. We were permitted to take all our little personal effects, but as none of us were possessed of a great quantity of goods this favor was not of much value to us.

Some of us had blankets and overcoats; some had neither. Many had parted with their clothing from time to time for something to eat, and many of this class had barely clothing to hide their nakedness and not enough for their comfort, even in that mild climate.

We were loaded into box cars, about sixty or seventy in a car, and this necessitated considerable crowding. We passed a number of towns and villages on the route, the names of which I cannot recall. We traveled all night after leaving Danville, only stopping now and then to let other trains pass and to procure water. Our crowded condition made the trip tiresome and disagreeable, but we endured it patiently, hoping that a change to a new prison would bring us relief in some way.

The second day out our train collided with another train loaded with negroes. The engines were badly crushed, but no one on board was injured. We were delayed several hours while procuring another engine and again we moved on. During the second night we halted near a village of considerable size. Here we got off the train and spent the night in camp near the track. I was so worn out with travel that I did not care to make an attempt to escape, but slept soundly all night.

Next morning we again moved on our way and late in the day passed through Macon, in the state of Georgia, and the same night reached Andersonville, a station about sixty miles south of Macon. We remained in the cars till daylight and were then unloaded and had a small supply of food issued to us. This consisted of cornbread and meat, but miserable in quality and meager in quantity. Following the advice of an inspired writer, we ate what was set before us and asked no questions. Andersonville consisted of a few railroad buildings and about a half dozen dwelling houses.

After we had eaten what had been furnished us we were ordered into line that a count might be made to ascertain if any had escaped. The commandant of the prison at this time was Captain Wirz, who for his inhuman brutality in the treatment of prisoners was afterward hung at Washington. Wirz was a devil in the shape of a man, a libel on the human race, and the date of his death ought to be celebrated all over the land with bonfires and illuminations. He came out of his quarters nearby, passed down our line with his hands clasped behind his back, eyeing us closely, but said not a word. He looked to be fifty-five years old, and had vicious, restless eyes sunk far into his head. He was tall and spare made with a slight stoop in his shoulders. He was not an American, but his looks gave him the appearance of a native of one of the German states. His look was cross, sour and forbidding, and he was altogether the fiend in appearance that he proved to be in fact.[2]

Before we were marched to the prison enclosure our names, companies and commands were carefully registered. The prison ground at this time contained about twelve thousand men and was situated nearly half a mile from the station. The prison was encircled by a stockade built by first digging a ditch four or five feet deep round the enclosure. Into this ditch were planted heavy hewn timbers, reaching above the surface twenty feet, and firmly set in the ditch with dirt packed in closely to hold them in their place, firm and solid.

On top of this stockade, at a distance of twenty yards from each

Captain Henry Wirz, commandant of Andersonville's prison stockade from March 1864 to April 1865. Unlike the impeccable attire he donned for this photograph believed taken in Europe during the summer of 1863, Wirz frequently "bustled about the prison in a white linen shirt and white duck trousers, with a revolver strapped to his side and a gray army cap drawn squarely over his eyebrows as token uniform."

Library of Congress

other, was a number of platforms, or sentry posts, where the guards were stationed when on duty, and on the outside at each platform was a rude stairway which led from the ground to the platform, and which was for the purpose of assisting the guard to reach his post of duty. On the inside of the stockade, at a distance of ten feet from and parallel with it, ran the "dead line."

This dead line was a row of posts set in the ground at intervals of ten or twelve feet apart, on the tops of which a narrow plank was nailed. The guards were instructed to shoot any prisoner who should approach nearer to the stockade than this line. A small stream of water ran through the stockade near the center. From this stream the prisoners procured all the water they used. This was warm and disagreeable to the taste and really was unfit for use.[3] A few trees grew in the enclosure, and the stumps of many more were to be seen here and there.

When we entered the stockade the men already there flocked around us and asked a multitude of questions concerning our capture and imprisonment, and many other questions concerning the progress of the war, which we could not answer. We were not supplied with tents or any other means of protection after coming here, and the supply of such things which we brought with us was totally insufficient for our actual needs. We were, therefore, left to shift for ourselves in this matter, each man as a rule taking care of himself in the construction of his habitation.

Sometimes a number of men would associate together in a club and by each contributing a piece of tent, a bit of blanket or cloth, they managed to provide better means of shelter than could have been done singly. But there were many who had nothing of any kind out of which to construct what might shelter them from the scorching sun by day or the chilly air by night. To this class the burning sun and heavy dews added much to their other hardships.

Four other prisoners joined me in the construction of quarters and we chose a location in the eastern part of the stockade only a few feet from the dead line and on the south side of the creek. We dug down into the sand nearly two feet, and with our blankets and some pieces of canvas which one of our number was fortunate enough to have in his possession, we managed to construct a very respectable looking tent compared with the others about us. There was a guard post opposite to where we had located our tent. This spot had been selected by us on account of its commercial advantages, for being thus situated we could trade with the guards when any trading was to be done.

Before leaving Danville I had taken the precaution to lay in a stock of tobacco, and in fixing up our tent I placed the tobacco nearby where it attracted the attention of a prisoner passing by. He inquired to know if I would sell it, and at what price. I told him I would take a dollar a plug for it, and he said that he would take it all at that price. I declined to sell it all at that time, but allowed him to take three plugs, for which he paid me three dollars in greenbacks. Another prisoner standing by said to me that I could have got three dollars a plug for it as well as one dollar. I thought this very strange, for this same tobacco could be bought at Danville for twenty-five cents a plug. I now began to realize that prices ranged much higher here than at Danville.

Soon after this first sale a guard came on duty at the post nearest our tent with a bunch of onions for sale. These I bought and placed them in small piles for sale again. In a short time I had sold seven dollars worth of onions and still had some left for our own use, which made us a light mess. Our previous prison experience had taught us valuable lessons of economy, and every atom of food was made to answer to its fullest extent.

Our arrival at Andersonville was about the middle of May 1864, and the weather was already oppressively warm.[4] Being unaccustomed to the climate of this latitude we suffered more from heat than we otherwise would have done.

Our rations at first consisted of about two-thirds of a pint of unsifted corn meal, a half pint of raw beans and a small piece of meat; the latter, however, we did not receive but two days out of three. We drew our rations at ten or eleven in the forenoon; then having to cook them we could not get our dinner sooner than about one o'clock. Though the rations we drew were designed by our captors to make us three meals, we invariably ate the whole quantity for one, and if this one meal had been sufficient to satisfy our appetites we would have thought ourselves fortunate.

Wood for cooking purposes was a scarce article, and to procure enough for our needs we dug the roots from the ground, hacked up the stumps and it was not long until every stump, root, chip and splinter within the stockade had been gathered and consumed. In cooking we usually boiled our beans first till they were soft; then our meat was sliced thin and put in; afterwards our meal was added and stirred, making what we called "loblolly." When a number messed and cooked together the food was carefully divided, giving to each man his exact share of the mess.

My first trade with the guards having resulted so favorably, I determined to continue to traffic with the guards who came on duty at the post nearest our tent, and besides furnishing our mess with something extra I soon began to accumulate money ahead.

Additional prisoners were being brought in nearly every day. These had more or less money, and while their money lasted they bought whatever they could find to eat, regardless of the price. Anything fit to eat sold at fabulous prices, and tobacco was not an exception. The following prices were obtained: three flour biscuits, $1.00; three eggs, $1.00; a pint of flour, $1.00; onions ranged from 75 cents to $1.25

each; fresh pork, $2.00 a pound; potatoes were bought off the guards at $35 a bushel, and afterward retailed singly; coffee brought $5 per pound. These prices were on a greenback basis, Confederate money being at ten cents on the dollar.

The daily additions being made to our numbers soon brought on a crowded condition of the prison, resulting in much discomfort and additional suffering. In a vast crowd like this there are always a variety of characters, and it may not seem strange that vice in its worst forms should have representatives, and that the depraved and baser elements in such a multitude should assert themselves. Here was the sneak thief, the gambler, the highwayman, the murderer — experts in every vice in the catalogue, and these made it necessary to keep a careful watch on everything of value, night and day. Theft, robbery and other heinous crimes were committed in open day and were alarmingly frequent.

There were two main streets running through the prison grounds — one on the north side and one on the south, the creek running between the two. These streets on either side were lined with the tradesmen who bought from the guards in large quantities and afterward retailed in smaller quantities to their fellow prisoners. These dealers occupied small stands at various places all over the ground.[5]

At one place could be seen a dealer selling flour at a dollar a pint; near him could be seen the dealer in onions and potatoes. Another one could be seen at another place with eggs, biscuits and the like. The lowest class of merchants dealt in soup bones. After first being carefully picked, these bones were sawed or cut into small pieces so as to show the marrow to advantage. Then some wretched soldier, hatless, his pants worn off to the knees and his shirt sleeves worn off to the elbows, would take these bones and, standing in a commanding position, would yell out at the top of his voice: "Here is your nice, fine, rich soup bones for sale. Walk right up and buy the best."

My numerous trades with the guards resulted in my becoming personally known to many of them, and this was a great advantage to us in our provision traffic. By careful buying and selling I not only kept the mess constantly supplied with many extras, but had accumulated over two hundred dollars. I had been singularly prosperous in all I had undertaken.

The grounds were becoming more and more crowded every day,

for hardly a day passed that did not add to our numbers, and as the season advanced the weather became excessively hot and much sickness was the result. The water which we were compelled to drink and make general use of was warm and dirty. There was always a large number of men at the creek washing and getting water, and the consequence was that the water was made unfit for use except for washing. This led to the digging of wells in various parts of the grounds. The surface being sandy for fifteen or twenty feet made digging quite easy and better water was reached at a depth of twenty-two feet than could be had at the creek. Many of these wells, however, soon became useless by caving in.

Our supply of fuel had become exhausted; every tree, stump and root had been used and now and then small squads were allowed to go out under guard to bring in a supply of wood. Going out for wood was considered quite a favor, and he who happened to be so fortunate as to be detailed for that purpose was to be congratulated, for in so doing he found many an opportunity of getting some nice bit to eat in some manner or other. Or, if he failed in this, he could breathe the pure air and rest his wearied eyes on green fields and listen to the songs of the free, happy birds. On such occasions he was wont to wish that he had the wings of the wind that he might fly away to a land of beauty, wealth and happiness, leaving behind the horrid scenes of that worse than horrid prison pen.

The prevailing diseases among the sick were scurvy and chronic diarrhea, and to such an extent had these and other complaints grown that the hospitals on the outside were sufficient for the accommodation of less than one-fourth of those who needed such accommodation, and consequently hundreds, for lack of needed attention and medical treatment, were left to die inside of the stockade.[6]

Each morning the bodies of such that had died during the preceding night were carried out to the dead-house. Here they were piled in wagons like so many logs of wood and hauled to the place of burial, where they were placed side by side in long, deep trenches and covered with dirt. No such thing as a coffin or box was used to enclose the bodies and their funeral rites were things only to be thought of, but not to be observed. The Union prisoners were employed in the work of digging these trenches and covering up their dead comrades. Even the duty of carrying a dead comrade outside of the stockade was esteemed a favor, and I have known men to pay $5 for the privilege of carrying a corpse to the dead-house. The reason of this was that in returning from such duty each man was permitted to bring in a load of wood for his own benefit.

Notwithstanding the prevailing death rate, our prison continued to become more and more crowded and the whole available space inside the dead line was taken up. The whole area became a moving mass of struggling, suffering humanity. We were so densely packed that in attempting to move around we had to pick our way with caution through the throng. The grounds were at length enlarged by the addition of eight acres to the enclosure, making the total area near twenty acres, and yet this addition, though it gave us some relief, still left us very much crowded.[7]

By July 1st 1864, it was estimated that our numbers reached twenty-five thousand, a figure rather below than above the real number, I have no doubt. With increasing numbers the morals of the prison seemed to become more and more corrupt. Person and property were safe nowhere. Robberies and petty thievery occurred day and night. No one was safe from the attacks of the human vultures who preyed upon their weaker and more unfortunate brethren.

About the first of July our captors began cooking our rations on the outside of the prison, thus avoiding the necessity of sending us out for wood under guard. Instead of corn meal, as before, we received corn-bread made from unsifted meal and without salt. Our beans also were cooked for us, and about every other day we were furnished with a very small bit of meat to each man. It is truly astonishing what a small quantity of food it takes to sustain human life, and how tenaciously we cling to life, even when it seems to offer nothing but suffering. Our circumstances illustrated this point to an extent we never before dreamed of.

We had among us men of all grades and dispositions. All the walks of life had representatives, and misery and wretchedness paid no respect to one more than to the other. Squalid misery stalked abroad at midday, nor stayed its hand in the darkness of night. Men who had been brought up in affluence and elegance shared the wretchedness of the lowest born of his comrades. The poorer and most destitute — those without tents, blankets or other means of comfort — wandered about the pen seeking stray crumbs of food that might fall their way. Old potato parings, stray beans or any other morsel were eagerly sought and devoured. Their sharpened visages and haggard looks told a tale of starvation and want that cannot be expressed by tongue or pen. To alleviate the sufferings of those around us seemed next to impossible. We were all in the same desperate condition, and if there were those who seemed to fare better than the rest, they were such as resorted to trade and made special efforts to improve their condition. An effort to relieve one would cause a thousand others, as destitute as the one, to ask for relief on as good grounds.

On the south side of the creek the grounds had become very miry. The filth from the higher grounds had accumulated in this quarter and it became a quagmire. Millions of maggots squirmed and worked in this filthy offal, presenting a sight which, when seen, can never be recalled except with a shudder of disgust.

Constant association with sickness, suffering and death had made us somewhat callous in our feelings toward our fellow sufferers, and many had allowed this feeling of indifference to take full possession of them, leaving no room for sympathy or pity. With each of us it was such a struggle for existence that self-preservation ruled our every act and dictated our very thoughts. The weaker and more destitute were the first victims of disease and death. It seemed in many cases that when hunger and disease had done their work, the starving victim would wander off to the creek and there he would fall, or, sinking into the swampy soil, would there lay until death overcame him. No helping hand reached out to aid him. Every finer and nobler feeling seemed paralyzed, and the one thought of self-preservation checked every feeling of humanity. Death was doing its work on the right and on the left, and it was a common thing to pass by a dying man in our walks around the different parts of the prison. Lying in the hot sun, unattended and usually unknown, the sufferer would struggle with the grim monster until struggling ended in surrender. Hundreds were passing by but no one cared to waste his time or his pity on a dying man.

Inspectors passed through our prison nearly every day making search for any attempt at tunneling out that we might make, and if a tunnel was begun it was usually detected before progressing far. One tunnel, however, escaped detection and this was projected about twenty yards from the stockade. A party of prisoners was pretending

Courtesy of Larry M. Strayer

Private Edwin W. Niven

A. Lincoln Presidential Center

Private Edwin W. Elliott

Michael C. Wright Collection

Private George Bailey

Det Femtende Regiment Wisconsin Frivillige

Private Ole Peterson

to be engaged in digging a well, and after reaching a depth of fifteen feet a tunnel was begun and pushed vigorously toward the outer side of the stockade. When the inspectors made their daily rounds the diggers would be found in the bottom of their well hard at work, and the inspectors looked in approvingly or passed on without suspicion of the scheme at hand. The work progressed undiscovered by the rebels until the workmen had passed under the stockade, and preparations were being made for a grand exit in a short time. Unluckily for the enterprise, the two men who were working in it one morning about sunup struck too near the surface and the earth's crust caved in on them. Being on the outside they sprang out and ran for life and liberty. They were seen by the guards who fired many times at them, but so far as we could see they were unhurt and I never learned of their recapture.

Now and then some poor, unfortunate prisoner would wander unthinkingly over the dead line and suffer the consequences, for the established rule was to shoot the offender without warning — a rule that was enforced with fiendish delight by some of our guards. How many met death in this way I know not, but the number was not a few. Some of the guards would fire on a prisoner whenever they could find any kind of an excuse for so doing, but others were more humane and only enforced the rigorous rules of the prison because it was their duty.

Before the middle of July the number of prisoners at Andersonville exceeded twenty-five thousand, and with increasing numbers the want, destitution, sickness and death grew more and more dreadful.

Mention has been previously made of the moral depravity and

OPPOSITE: *All four of these young Union soldiers perished in Camp Sumter's stockade during the summer of 1864 and are buried in the cemetery at Andersonville National Historic Site. Captured November 15, 1863, near Woodville, Ala., Edwin Niven, Company I, 3rd Ohio Cavalry, died June 15. George Bailey, Company A, 72nd Indiana Mounted Infantry, was captured in February 1864 at Okolona, Miss., and succumbed to scurvy and starvation August 8. Edwin Elliott, Company B, 92nd Illinois Mounted Infantry, died September 7 after five months in captivity. Ole Peterson, an original member of Company I, 15th Wisconsin, was captured May 27, 1864, near New Hope Church, Ga., and died September 21.*

consequent crimes resulting from time to time. Robberies were occurring daily and it was apparent that measures must be taken to bring the offenders to justice. But how to proceed to reach that end was a question not easily answered and for a time we endured what we could not remedy. Money grew scarcer and scarcer, for the reason that it was being continually sent outside the prison and none of it was being returned. This state of affairs was aggravated by the fact that it was becoming almost impossible to trade with the guards. The prison authorities finally established a trading post inside the prison and here we were compelled to do whatever trading we did do, but as very few of the prisoners had any money our patronage to the established store was exceedingly light.

Up to the time at which our trading with the guards was prohibited I had, from a small beginning, increased my capital to two hundred and forty dollars, besides expending a large amount for such extras as money would buy. But now my money began to decrease, for every day I was put to some expense without any income and under this state of things my money was rapidly disappearing.

Among the prisoners in the stockade there were about thirty negroes; these were taken out daily to perform labor on the outside and were brought in at night. With a view to replenishing my wasted finances I gave one of these colored men forty-five dollars, telling him to buy with it anything that could be eaten and bring it into the prison with him, and that I would pay him for all his trouble. This he agreed to do. That night when the colored squad was brought in I went to their quarters and found the man with whom I had entrusted my money, and made inquiry of his success. He reported that he had purchased several articles of food with the money, but that the Confederate guards at the gate had forced him to give it all to them. Here was forty-five dollars gone at one fell swoop, and my spirits fell to a low state.

I waited several days, and seeing no other means of renewing my trade I gave fifteen dollars to another man of the colored squad, instructing him to buy and bring in something to eat. But he came in with a report similar to the first, bringing back neither food nor money. Not caring to invest further in this line of speculation, I gave up further effort and waited for something to turn up, contenting myself by economizing the money I had remaining as well as I could.

The adage "misfortunes come in pairs" now verified itself, for following the loss of my money I was attacked with scurvy, a disease that already had carried to the grave hundreds of my fellow prisoners. Very few who were victims of scurvy ever recovered, and I naturally supposed I would go with the majority. Our situation was such that it was nearly impossible to procure the necessary remedies for the disease; therefore, when a man was taken down with the scurvy he usually remained in his tent or laid out in the open air unattended till he died.

Captain Wirz, who had charge of the prison, usually rode through the stockade twice a day, but none of the prisoners were allowed to speak to him during these visits, and we were even denied the right to represent our grievances in a petition to our friends or our enemies. Misery and suffering that cannot be told was our common lot, and though it be retold a thousand times there remains that which is too shocking to tell and too inhuman to be believed. Death was making rapid inroads in our ranks every day, for at least fifty were carried to the graveyard every day. It was a common sight to see men lying in the hot sand, forsaken and alone, unable to help themselves, sweltering in the burning sun and slowly but surely dying.

We were forsaken, even by those who should have been our friends, for our government at Washington, by the advice and policy of Secretary [of War Edwin M.] Stanton, refused to exchange us or to give an equal number of rebel prisoners for us in return; for they said in effect: "We will not give healthy, robust Confederates in our hands who are fit for the front for a like number of half-starved and half-dead men who will never be fit for service. It is policy to let them stay where they are, even if they should all die." This might have been "policy," but to say the least it was very heartless policy.[8]

Crime of various kinds continued to grow more and more frequent; indeed it became known that an organized band existed in the prison, the object of which was plunder. This band numbered several hundred, and its members pledged to support and protect each other from any punishment resulting from their misdemeanors. Now and then one of the band would be caught in some offense and would be punished by the shaving of one side of his head; sometimes bucking was added to the punishment. But it appeared that the principals were never caught in this way. If they were detected in their deeds they seemed to be strong enough to defy punishment. It was the little, one-horse starveling who was caught and made to suffer. The arrival of fresh prisoners generally was followed by a series of robberies, for this class of men brought into the prison more or less money and the thieves usually fell upon them and rendered them penniless, sometimes beating them besides. On one occasion a newly arrived prisoner showed desperate resistance when attacked by members of the gang, and the result was he was very dangerously beaten by the freebooters.

This brutal act created a feeling of indignation on the part of the order-loving prisoners. But being weak, half-starved, unorganized and each man compelled to make a desperate effort to support life, he had little thought of redressing the wrongs of others so long as he himself remained unmolested. And thus three or four hundred desperadoes, well organized, were able to hold in awe the other thousands who loved peace and good order.

Following the beating above mentioned it was resolved that further forbearance would only result in greater outrages, and therefore a few of us determined to draw up and sign a petition to Wirz setting forth the state of affairs of outlawry as it existed in the stockade. We prevailed on a Confederate lieutenant to bear our petition to Captain Wirz, asking that immediate attention be given the same. The next day Wirz and several other Confederate officers came into the stockade and held several conferences with the prisoners in various parts of the grounds, making diligent inquiry into the nature of the offenses and, as far as possible, trying to ascertain the number and names of the offenders. Such information was furnished as fully satisfied them that the complaints in our petition were properly founded.

On the following day a Confederate captain and lieutenant came into the enclosure with a detachment of soldiers, armed and equipped. A police force of near four hundred of the honest prisoners was then detailed and organized. Then a call was made to all who were in any way acquainted with the facts concerning the commission of crimes to come forward and make them known.

Now that they were to be protected there were plenty of witnesses and no lack of testimony touching the outrages. These proceedings came upon the thieves unexpectedly and caused them great consternation. They had not expected this righteous outburst of long-delayed retribution and knew not what to do. The worst of them were hunted in every part of the prison. The robber element had suddenly come to grief. More than forty of the ringleaders and principals were arrested and taken outside the prison under a strong guard.

Here the trial was held. Captain Wirz said to us: "Now, you can try these men in your own way, and if they be found guilty of the crimes of which they stand charged, they shall suffer just punishment and you shall be protected in your decision."

A jury of twelve was then impaneled from among the prisoners and a judge, having the proper legal qualifications to decide the points of law which might arise, also was chosen. The accused were provided with good counsel and the prosecution was conducted by legal talent of no ordinary kind.

The trial then proceeded, being on the outside of the prison and under a strong Confederate guard.[9] It was characterized by great fairness and impartiality. The accused had an array of testimony to prove their innocence, but with every effort that could be brought forth on their behalf there was much damaging testimony given against them. At the close of the trial the jury retired twenty-four hours, and upon being called for a verdict they decided that thirty-five of the accused should run the gauntlet on the inside of the stockade, and that six of the number, whom they found by the evidence to be the principals, should be publicly hanged.

The punishment by running the gauntlet took place immediately and those who were to suffer in this manner were divided into two parties, with one party taken to each of the two main entrances to the stockade. Here were ranged long lines of prisoners on either side of a space a few feet in width and extending far into the prison grounds. As the culprits ran between these lines they were pelted, kicked and otherwise assaulted by such of the prisoners as were quick enough to reach them. Many of the offenders were badly beaten and it was rumored that two of them died from the effects of their injuries.

Those who were condemned to suffer death by hanging were allowed ten days of preparation to meet their fate, but they were kept under a strong guard [in stocks] outside the prison during this time. Thieves from this time forward fared roughly, for the prisoners were now well organized, having a police force of four hundred men that diligently sought out and arrested any prisoner reported guilty of crime. When it became known that sure and severe punishment would follow the commission of a crime, the offenses from which the inoffensive and helpless ones suffered grew very rare.

The scurvy from which I had been suffering grew worse and I was now barely able to walk about, but I tried to keep my spirits up and made strong efforts to continue on my feet, for I felt that if I once gave up I should certainly die. The scurvy affected us in two different forms: In one class of cases the limbs of the patient would swell and become a dark crimson color, and if the swollen flesh was pressed with the finger the impress would remain for some time. In the other cases the flesh hardened and shrank up, turning to a dark brown color. The sense of feeling was lost in some cases. In the last named cases the flesh would feel like hard, dry wood, and the joints would be more or less swelled. In both cases the gums swelled and the teeth became loose. My case was the last described kind, which was called the bone scurvy.

On the day set apart for the execution of the six robbers I was barely able to move about with the aid of a cane, but the excitement of the occasion helped me to greater activity than for several days previous.

The scaffold on which the execution was to take place was erected on the inside of the prison and near the southern gate. When the hour arrived I hobbled out to that part of the grounds and took a position about fifteen yards from the scaffold. Nearly twenty-five thousand prisoners were looking on in solemn silence, and the scene was too impressive ever to be forgotten.

The doomed men were brought in under a strong guard of Confederate soldiers and were then delivered to the prisoners to be executed. The guards now retired to the outside, leaving the condemned men in the hands of the organized force of prisoners. Not a Confederate remained to witness the execution. It was indeed a painfully solemn thing to see these six men in the prime of life, surrounded by such misery and wretchedness, thus to suffer the penalty which their dark deeds had brought upon them. They were brought in with their hands tied behind them, attended by a Catholic priest who offered them the consolation of their religion in their last hours.[10]

When the time came and they were commanded to mount the scaffold, one of them, a large and powerful man, exclaimed to the others: "I can never stand this," and with a sudden and powerful effort burst the cords that bound him and made a desperate dash for his life.

In a moment all was confusion and excitement. Only those in the immediate vicinity of the scaffold comprehended what was going on. Even where I stood I could not at first understand the cause of the consternation. The impression prevailed with many of the prisoners that the rebels were about to fire upon us from their batteries situated on the higher grounds commanding the prison, and which were kept ready for use in case of an attempted mass breakout.

The excitement reached a high pitch. Two men standing near me jumped down a well eighteen feet deep to escape the destruction which they imagined awaited us all, but as soon as we ascertained that the confusion arose from the effort of one man trying to escape, quiet was somewhat restored. This man, whose name was Curtis, parted the crowd in front of him, flinging the men right and left in his madness and desperation. He was followed by the organized police and a large crowd of the prisoners. He ran to the eastern part of the stockade, and in attempting to cross the creek he sank up to his waist in the filthy offal. He was now captured and brought back. He must have known the impossibility of escaping under such circumstances, and it is a wonder that any man of ordinary judgment would have attempted such a thing.

Soon after he was brought back the six were marched to their places on the fatal platform from which they were to be launched into eternity. They were still attended by the priest who continued to counsel with and pray for them.

I remember well the remark made by Curtis just before the drop fell. He said, "It was my old grandmother who said I would die with my boots on, and I guess it is coming to pass." Finally, when all was ready, the priest retired from the scaffold and meal sacks were drawn over the heads of the condemned men, as black caps are on such occasions under other circumstances. The trap sprung and five of the six were soon lifeless. The sixth man in his fall broke the rope and tumbled to the ground. He begged piteously for his life, telling his executioners that the breaking of the rope was proof of his innocence. But his begging was all in vain and availed nothing. He was again made to mount the scaffold and in brief time was sent to bear his guilty companions company. Their bodies were taken down inside of an hour and received proper burial.

These executions took place July 11, 1864. The men executed were John Sarsfield, 140th N.Y. Infantry, William Collins, 88th Pa. Infantry, Pat Delaney, 83d Pa. Vols., Charles Curtis, 5th R.I. [Heavy Artillery], A[ndrew] Muir, U.S. Navy and W.R. Rickson, U.S. Navy.*

The executions had their desired effect; they not only disposed of the principal criminals who had terrorized the prison but restrained others from the commission of crime. From this time forward there was little theft or outlawry compared with the times preceding the executions. Captain Wirz should have credit for the part he took in bringing about this reform.

My health grew worse from day to day, the scurvy gaining continually and my vitality and strength weakening proportionately. New prisoners had nearly ceased to be brought in and a general impression prevailed that we were soon to be moved away. Money had become very scarce with all the men. My funds had dwindled from day to day and the future looked darker than at any time since coming here.

It is worthy of particular mention that of all the religious creeds of the land, the Catholics were the only ones who visited us in our misery or seemed touched at our condition. The priests of this church came into our prison every day, rain or shine, and ministered as best they could to the wants of the most destitute, but where there were so many in need it was next to impossible to do much. The worst cases were helped to a few delicacies and comforted in various ways.

The Masons of Albany, a place fifty miles south of Andersonville, brought much relief to those of their order among us. Many a member

---

* W.R. Rickson was an alias for Charles Curtis. The sixth man hung was John Sullivan, 76th New York Infantry. All except Muir were Union army deserters. Muir had been a seaman aboard the Federal steamer *Water Witch* when it was boarded and captured south of Savannah, Ga., during the early morning hours of June 3, 1864. Entering Andersonville prison stockade on June 7, Muir was incarcerated less than five weeks before his hanging. [William Marvel, *Andersonville: The Last Depot* (Chapel Hill: The University of North Carolina Press, 1994), p. 70, 94, 275].

National Archives

An Andrew J. Riddle photograph believed taken August 16, 1864, showing Andersonville's open latrine and unchanneled eastern end of "Stockade Creek." That month nearly 33,000 prisoners were packed into the stockade's 26 and a half acres.

of that mystic tie was helped to a clean shirt, a pair of shoes or something to eat by the Masonic brethren.

About the first of September 1864 the Confederates began moving some of our number away.[11] Everybody was anxious to go first, for we had seen and suffered so much here that it seemed to us that any place on earth besides this would be better. I was too sick at this time to care for myself and was therefore a burden to my companions, several of whom made many sacrifices for my comfort and relief. The fact that my money was nearly all gone added to my misery, for even in prison money is not to be despised. I suffered much pain in my limbs at night, and as a consequence I slept but little. I was continually tormented by a thousand doubts and uncertainties which kept me in a constant state of restlessness, from which I had no relief.

It was estimated that during the months of July and August the deaths averaged one hundred and fifty daily.[12] Our numbers were being reduced daily, both by deaths and removals, so that this was some relief even to those who remained, for it gave us more room and better and purer air to breathe.

About the 10th of September the prisoners constituting our division were called on to leave. This occasioned much shouting and other demonstrations of joy, but being entirely unable to move from my tent it brought grief to me instead of joy, for knowing that my companions would have to go I realized that I would be left unattended and would surely suffer for care which none would be willing and few able to give. It was of no use to depend on strangers for care unless I could pay them, and I lacked the money to do that, having now only sixty-five cents in postal currency.

My fortunate comrades, before leaving me, brought me a quantity of fresh water and arranged my blankets on sticks in such a manner as to protect me from the sun. Having done all in their power to leave me comfortable they bade me an affectionate farewell, and I could see by their manner that they expected I would not recover, and that a few days at most would end all with me. Following their departure I felt very lonely and my spirits were much depressed. I now had no helping hands to minister to me, for, though I was surrounded by the multitude I was almost as much alone as if I had been on the desert of Sahara. I had seen hundreds lying alone and slowly dying, friendless and uncared for, and I now felt that I was surely in the same desolate condition.

That evening I prevailed on a prisoner to bring me some fresh water and as darkness came on I pulled my blanket from the sticks and wrapped it about me as best I could and tried to sleep, but being full of pain and direful apprehensions I slept but little. I had no appetite and what rations I drew were nauseating to my taste — the sight of them was unpleasant in the extreme. I grew careless concerning my rations and cared little whether I received my scanty portion or not.

The next morning after my comrades left me, as the sun rose and its rays began to scorch me, I tried several times to get some passing prisoners to fix up my blanket in the form of a shelter as on the previous day, but all were too busy or too heartless to give any attention to a dying man. At length I prevailed on one man to bring me some fresh water and fix up my tent by giving him my rations for the day. During the day I was visited by a Catholic priest who gave me half a lemon, which greatly refreshed me for a short time. I now thought my days were numbered and concluded that I could live but a few days at farthest. But the outlook, gloomy as it was, had some relief in it, for I felt that death would be preferable to such a life as I had been living for weeks in the past.

The day wore away and night — a dreadful night — came on. A terrible storm of rain, thunder and wind raged for hours, and being compelled to lie on the wet ground unprotected I was thoroughly drenched and slept but little, and that little was full of frightful dreams and brought me little rest. I wished I might fall asleep and never waken. Morning came at last and the burning sun drove its scorching heat into my weak and emaciated flesh. I became delirious as the day advanced and continued so till toward evening, and when I recovered consciousness I found that I had been carried during the day to the northern part of the stockade and placed in a long shed which had recently been erected.[13]

The sick and dying lay about me in great numbers. Many were on the outer side of the shed waiting to take the places of those who were being carried to the dead-house from within. I well remember my feelings when, on regaining consciousness, I looked around me and beheld the terrible scene by which I was surrounded. I determined to make a desperate effort to live and therefore set my will in an attitude of defiance toward the grim monster.

Next to me on my right lay a tall and large-framed man having on a red shirt. This man was delirious and was talking wildly and without meaning. I remember how I shuddered when I beheld the vast number of lice with which his body was covered. It appeared to me that there were thousands of them of all sizes, from huge old plump ones down to the tiny midget of an hour old. The poor man soon surrendered and the battle for life was at an end, for on the next morning I found him stiff and silent. I had slept but little during the night, for the continued moaning of the sick made sleep next to impossible.

With the return of light came renewed hopes and a still greater desire to live. I was now furnished with some corn meal and beans, but being helpless it was not possible for me to cook them, and besides I had no appetite notwithstanding I had eaten nothing for several days. But I was convinced that I must eat something to sustain life, for I must soon die of starvation unless I did. So I gave my meal and beans to a well prisoner to cook on the halves, and when it was cooked I ate a part of it, which was very little. Yet I still believe that in thus forcing myself to eat what I could proved to be the means by which the brittle thread of life was saved from breaking.

I desired to be taken out of the prison and placed in the hospital on the outside. I spent the day in planning to this end, for it was my only hope of life. Numbers of the sick were being taken to the hospital each day for treatment, and it appeared to me that if I could only get out of the stockade and into the hospital I should recover.

The next morning I told the prisoner who had cooked and shared my rations on the previous day that, if he would carry me down to the gate where the negroes came with wagons daily for the sick, he might have all my rations for that day. This he promised to do if he could get his partner to assist him. He then went in search of his partner; presently they both came and carried me to the gate. At the gate were a great many sick all waiting for their turn to be taken to the hospital. The two men who carried me to the gate laid me in the shade of a canvas tent occupied by some of the under-officials of the prison. They then went their way. When the wagons came I yelled with all my strength and asked to be loaded in, but no one paid any attention to me. So the wagons were driven away with their load, leaving me and others behind. I learned that in two hours the wagons would return for another load, so I comforted myself with the hope that I might yet get to go.

When the wagons returned I begged to be put into one of them, but the result was the same as before and again the wagons were driven away, leaving me dejected and almost hopeless. Let me try ever so hard, someone was always ready to step in and take my place.

I was told that the wagons would return for one more load that day and I again began planning to try and make the trip. I had a ring of rare value, one I had taken from home when I enlisted, and for various reasons I prized it very dearly and had always intended to keep it in remembrance of its donor. But now I was on the verge of death, as I thought, and I felt justified in sacrificing the ring for my own benefit. I therefore bargained with an Irishman, promising him the ring if he

Prisoners are issued rations just inside the stockade's north gate at Anderson-ville, August 16, 1864.

would put me in one of the wagons when they came.

It was near sundown when the wagons arrived for their last load, and faithful to his agreement the Irishman picked me up and put me in one of the wagons, and we were driven away. Many were left behind who, like myself, were desirous of getting to the hospital, but as there were accommodations for only so many, some must be left for another day when as many could be taken from the stockade as would fill the places of those who had died on the previous day. It was not every day that the wagons came for the sick, but only at times when the deaths in the hospital made it possible to accommodate more. So if we missed getting out on the day the sick were hauled out we must wait until another favorable day. This might be the next day, or it might be several days. In this interval many would die.

The hospital was located [southeast] from the stockade and we reached it between sundown and dark. We were unloaded and a list of our names, companies and regiments taken. We were then put on wheelbarrows and wheeled to places to which we had been assigned. I was taken to a small wedge tent suitable for the accommodation of three persons. It already was occupied by one man, and he was sick nigh unto death.[14]

We were furnished with no special comforts. There were no beds or mattresses given us — nothing but the bare, sandy soil. Blankets were furnished to such prisoners as had none.

The hospital grounds contained six acres and were enclosed by a close board fence eight feet high. A line of sentries was stationed on three sides of the enclosure on the outside of the fence; on the south side the guards were on the inside. This was on account of the swampy condition of the land on this side. The grounds were carefully laid off, divided by streets and wards. The wards numbered from one to twenty.

A force of well prisoners was assigned to duty in the hospital and these men were required to keep the streets carefully swept and the whole grounds clear of offal. The tents used were of two kinds — the small wedge-shaped tent large enough for three persons, and the wall tent, which was large enough for twelve. The grounds were well shaded by trees, and altogether the hospital was a place of comfort and beauty compared to the stockade. Each ward had its ward-master and attendants to wait on the sick, but about all these did was to bring our rations to us.

Only one of many of our worst cases of sick recovered. The poor fellow who was in my tent when I first arrived soon died. Others were brought in from time to time and died, until nine had died by my side. During all this time I could not perceive that I was improving at all, nor did I seem to get worse. I bravely held my own from one day to another.

One or two days I was the only occupant of the tent. All my fellow sufferers died within a few days after being brought in from the stockade. Let it be remembered that though nine died in my tent, there was never more than three occupants at a time — myself and two others. This statement is difficult to believe, yet it is literally true. Of these cases one or two should have particular mention.

One was that of a large and well-framed man who was brought in late one evening. It had been raining hard and he was very wet. He was laid beside me and offered some food, which he refused, saying he did not feel like eating that evening and that he would save his rations till next morning. This man and myself were the only occupants of the tent that night. In the after part of the night he became very restless and annoyed me exceedingly by his rolling about, and by throwing himself against me so as to keep me from sleep. I became somewhat petulant and insisted upon his keeping his own side of the bed, and to cease from annoying me as he had been doing. To this he gave no heed, so getting hold of an old crutch which happened to be in the tent I placed it next to and under him so that it served as a prop to keep him in his part of the tent. After a time he became perfectly quiet and I supposed he had fallen asleep, and I was soon in dreamland myself. Upon awakening next morning I found that his was the sleep of death, and that his tossings which had annoyed me were the final struggles of the conflict between life and death.

Another case was that of a man who had been in the tent for a number of days, and who did not appear to be much sick so far as I could judge. He was able to get about much better than I could and had succeeded in crawling out of the tent to an oak tree which stood near. He took off his shirt and proceeded to hunt the lice off of it, a task of no small magnitude. He then began talking of his home and family, saying that if he could know that they were all comfortable and well provided for he could feel reconciled to his hard fate.

He continued to talk of his wife and children until I finally told him he was foolish to thus worry himself so about his family, and that their worst possible condition could hardly be a tenth as bad as his own, and that his best and wisest course would be to attend to his own wants as best he could, and that doubtless his family was being properly cared for by friends at home. The poor man paid very little attention to my advice but continued to worry and fret as before, until all of a sudden, and apparently without a pain or struggle, he expired.

It was a great surprise to me; I had no idea that death was so near. I saw many, very many die in a similar manner. It seemed that men died without realizing the approach of the grim monster, and also appeared that long-continued suffering in mind and body had made them callous to pain, and that when the final moment came they ceased to live much as a lighted candle is extinguished by a gust of wind. Hope had fed the flickering flame from day to day and, more dead than alive, they moved about vainly chasing a phantom of release or exchange, a hope which lured from afar yet fled as they followed. Finally, when hope no longer cheered and when despair took the ascendancy, the victim surrendered and the wearied spirit forsook its prison-house of suffering and launched into the unknown sea of eternity.

Our daily rations in the hospital were a biscuit, a half pint of boiled rice and a bit of beef. As small and insufficient as this was, it was vastly better than we had been accustomed to receiving in the stockade. For a time after first entering the hospital I could hardly eat all my rations, but I forced myself to eat all they gave me, believing it really necessary to sustain life.

After the nine deaths had occurred in my tent, of which previous mention has been made, two patients were brought in from the stockade and assigned to my tent. These, contrary to the rule, did not die but began to improve, and this was an encouragement to me. I had seen so many die that I had come to look on death as a certain result of being assigned to my tent.

Seeing these companions improving day after day I seemed to take on new life and at once began to improve myself, and it was but a few days till we three were rapidly convalescing. My companions were both Dutchmen; their names were Edwards and Schrader. The former was a member of a Pennsylvania regiment and his home was at the town of Broadtop, Pa. Schrader was a native of Germany and a member of an Illinois regiment.[15]

The two men differed widely in their habits, characters and dispositions. Edwards was almost continually talking of his home, father, mother and two sisters; Schrader had little or nothing to say of his home or relatives. Edwards seldom washed his face or combed his hair, and I have known him to go for weeks with his face dirty and his hair matted. Schrader was tasty and careful in his personal habits, but was selfish and disagreeable. Edwards was tender-hearted and liberal. With all his slovenly personal habits he was much the better man of the two, but he had one weakness and that, under the circumstances, was a big disadvantage. He was a great glutton. It appeared that he had the capacity of half a dozen men for stowing away supplies. Nothing eatable ever went to waste where he was, and he never learned *division* as applied to anything fit to eat. His appetite may have been capable of being satisfied, but I do not remember that it ever was. We were all good eaters now and could have consumed much more than we received.

We were all improving and I began to hobble about on a crutch. The idea of dying in a rebel prison and of being buried in the sand of Georgia began to lose its grip on me. Our chief trouble was now, as it had been, to get enough to eat. Edwards was an expert beggar and was continually on the lookout for something to supply the mess with more than our drawn rations. Hardly a day passed that he did not beg something to eat from the attendants at the cook-house, and after filling himself I came in for the remainder. Schrader was crabbed and surly; he seldom had anything to do with Edwards or me, except that he slept in the same tent with us. Edwards and I frequently messed together. Schrader ate alone.

Each morning the bodies of those who had died during the previous night were deposited in the street preparatory to burial. From here they were wheeled to the dead-house and from thence they were taken in wagons to the place of burial. The dead averaged about thirty each morning.

My condition improved from day to day so that I was able to move about the hospital grounds by the aid of a crutch. I managed by a little trading to pick up something extra to eat. There were hundreds of sick and suffering fellows lying in their tents unable to help themselves, but who would get me to buy peanuts, yams and the like for them. I would take their money or other articles of value which they desired to exchange and, when opportunity offered, would sell them to the guards or exchange them for food and would be allowed a trifling commission for my trouble.

Notwithstanding the existence of an order against trading with our guards, we found many adroit ways and means of steering around the difficulties, and that necessity, which is said to be the mother of invention, was found to be the parent of many a shrewd scheme which brought relief to our urgent needs.

During the early period of our imprisonment at Andersonville there was a considerable amount of greenbacks among the prisoners, but now this money had disappeared almost entirely. Some of the men had small sums of postal currency. Confederate money was plenty enough, but it took a hundred dollars to buy a beef-head. Having little or no money to exchange with the guards for what we needed, we bartered articles of clothing, rings, trinkets, pocket-knives, &c., receiving beef-heads, pieces of beef, peanuts and yams. Our plans and bargains were made with the guards during the day, but the exchange of commodities had to be done at night and with the utmost caution to avoid being seen by the officers.

I had so far improved in my general health that I was on my feet and moving about during the entire day bargaining with the guards for such articles of food as could be smuggled through their hands and into ours during their hours of duty at night. In thus moving about I not only gained strength but my spirits improved, and I also was able to provide myself with about all I needed to eat.

In one of my night trades with a guard I came very near to losing my life. I had procured from a sick prisoner a nice gutta-percha pocket comb which opened and closed like a knife. This I offered to trade to a guard for peanuts. He prevailed on me, much against my better judgment, to allow him to take the comb to camp to show it to his lieutenant, promising faithfully to bring the pay for it that night at eleven o'clock when he again came on duty. When the hour arrived and the relief to which the guard properly belonged had been placed on their posts, I went down to that beat of the guard line where I expected to find the man who had taken the comb. I approached the sentry, and when within a few yards of him I spoke to him and inquired about our trade of the comb and peanuts. Instead of receiving a courteous answer, the guard said to me gruffly, "Now, you get away from here or I will put a ball through you," and as he ceased speaking he fired his piece at me with the evident purpose of furnishing the subject for a funeral on the following day. Though he failed in his plan I had no reason to censure him for his lack of skill as a marksman. Taking his advice I retired to my tent to ponder on the inhumanity of man to man and of the rascality of the rebel who had taken my comb with fraudulent intent, and who by trading off with another guard had not only cheated me out of my comb but had caused me to imperil my life, which in my improved state of health was becoming more and more valuable. The lesson was a useful one to me, for thereafter I planned so that no article passed out of my hands for inspection by a third party.

Shortly after this an affair occurred which more than set me even with my dishonest patrons. One of the guards wished to buy a pair of shoes, an article of which many of the soldiers of the C.S.A. stood much in need. He wanted a pair of pants also, and I promised to procure them for him, though at the time I did not know certainly that I could get them. He promised to give a shoulder of meat and five large yams for the shoes and pants, and the trade was to be consummated that night at eleven o'clock when he again came on guard at that post.

I hunted about during the afternoon among the sick, endeavoring to find the shoes and only partly succeeded. I found two good shoes, both for the left foot, one a No. 8 and the other No. 10. Even this assortment of stock caused me much effort, for I had to look through the camp before I found anyone willing to sell, as those who had good shoes and mates needed them too badly to part with them at any price which I could pay.

I put the shoes in as merchantable a shape as I could and felt that with a reasonably dark night to aid in the trade I might hope to succeed in convincing "Johnnie" that "shoes would be shoes" before the war was over. I found a pair of pants more readily than the shoes, and though they were not strictly No. 1 in quality, they were good enough to trade on by a little brushing up. When the hour arrived I repaired to the vicinity of the post we had agreed upon. At this place in the guard line the sentinels were stationed on the opposite side of the eight-foot-high plank fence. The night was somewhat dark and on that account more favorable for carrying out our purpose. We carried on a whispered conversation by means of a knot hole in a plank of the fence. There was mutual suspicion and a mutual lack of confidence on each side of the fence. The guard insisted that I should put the pants and shoes over the fence to him first, while I as stoutly insisted on his putting the meat and yams over to me first. I finally suggested to him that we put our articles over at the same time, one to the other. This he declined to do, saying that he feared the articles were not as represented. We would talk and parley awhile and then the guard would pace his beat, keeping up a show of duty, then he would return to the knot hole and the wrangle over the trade would be resumed.

Suddenly, while we were hotly engaged in our bantering and bad-gering, the "grand rounds" for the night, accompanied by the officers of the guard, came upon us. To escape detection the guard had but one thing to do. He threw the meat and yams over the fence to me and resumed his walk to halt the "grand rounds" party as he was required to do. I did not feel that I had any further business at that knot hole, so seizing the coveted prize I hied to my tent, not forgetting to take with me the shoes and pants, and congratulating myself on the success of my night's work.

I found Edwards at our tent patiently awaiting my return and in a good condition of appetite, as usual, to enjoy a feast. So we gathered together some wood splinters and proceeded to build a small fire, by means of which we soon fried a portion of the meat. The fire was in-sufficient to cook it thoroughly and we were at last compelled to eat it in a half-cooked condition, a circumstance which enabled us to bear valuable testimony on the superiority of rare pork over that which is well fried. We gorged ourselves completely and then slept peacefully, undisturbed by either stomach or conscience.

Whenever I had success in my undertakings, as in the above men-tioned case, I generally sought out my two comrades and shared with them the good results, even though Schrader was so surly and selfish that he never deserved it. Edwards very rarely succeeded in bringing in anything in this way, though once in a great while he made a good haul. Although Edwards seemed to have no faculty for trading, he once made a raise in the line of substance which deserves mention.

I was sitting in my tent one day engaged in putting a half-sole on the seat of my pants when Edwards came in with a well-filled haversack under his arm, looking as sneaking and guilty as if he had been caught robbing a savings bank. I inquired the cause of his singular conduct, but he said nothing very particular had occurred and then he hid the haversack and its contents under his blanket.

I knew something was wrong. After pressing him for an explana-tion he told me that the haversack contained a beef liver that he had got off one of the guards, whose post of duty was on the south side of the hospital grounds where the guard line was situated on the inside of the fence. I inquired of him how much he had paid for it, and his answer was that he had *promised* to pay the guard five dollars, and that though he had no money or any chances of paying for it, he was *so hungry* that he determined to take the liver anyhow and pay for it in promises. Edwards was an honest man, but his stomach had no regard for principle and sometimes led him into predicaments out of which it was difficult to rescue him. He was very ill at ease now that he had on his hands a case of liver complaint, for which the ordinary remedies were insufficient.

Knowing that I would share in the liver I engaged to share in my comrade's trouble concerning it. So telling him to remain in the tent I made my way down to the guard line, planning on my way how I might cancel the amount due the guard for the liver. I stood around near the guard for some time and then asked him if he had anything to trade or sell. He replied he did not, that he had just disposed of a beef liver to one of the prisoners and was now waiting for him to return the haversack and bring the money for the liver.

I then told the guard that a short time before I came down the doctors had arrested a fellow having a striped haversack which contained a liver, and that they had taken him to headquarters to tie him up by the thumbs until he would tell where and of whom he procured it. This statement, though not remarkable for its truthfulness, frightened the guard considerably. He said it must be the same one to whom he had sold the liver and that he feared the fellow would divulge the whole affair to the authorities, thereby bringing upon him some severe punishment. The guard then told me that if I would interest myself in his behalf by prevailing on the prisoner not to tell where he had got the liver, that he would not exact pay for it and that for my services in the case he would bring me four quarts of peanuts when he again came on guard. This I agreed to and, followed by the best wishes of the troubled sentry, I returned to the tent to share in a huge mess of boiled liver which Edwards had prepared during my absence — a mess the enjoyment of which was heightened rather than lessened by the wear and tear of conscience in procuring it.

I still kept up my trades with our guards and by this means we had our seasons of plenty now and then, though generally our supply of food was greatly below our needs and of a very inferior quality. I had bought an extra blanket and with the one I already had I was well provided in this particular.

Time dragged its slow length along. The dullest day had its sunset and the dreariest night was succeeded by the dawn of another day. Monotony was sometimes relieved by variety, and once in a while a gleam of hope's sunshine broke through the overhanging clouds of despair.

Many of the sick in our ward began to improve, but this was after more than fifty percent of the whole number had died. The prisoners had been removed from the stockade and distributed over different parts of the Confederacy, we knew not where. No more sick were being brought into the hospital as in former times, and many of the present occupants of the various wards were going about in improving health, performing light duties and giving to the hospital an air of life which was in happy contrast with the days gone by.

By the middle of December 1864 the only prisoners remaining at Andersonville were occupants of the hospital. No reliable news from the outside world touching the progress of the war reached us. Our captors seemed determined to withhold from us any news of the situation, as if our ignorance of passing events would increase the sufferings of our imprisonment. But our principal concern was to prolong our existence and to economize our scanty supplies so as to cheat the monster, grim-visaged death, of its prey.

Many deaths were still occurring among us, but they were much less frequent than before.[16] We had looked on death and suffering so long and so frequently that our feelings had grown callous and could witness scenes of horror with very little concern. When a patient died his effects were immediately taken possession of by his living comrades. In the possession of these effects many strange discoveries were made. One man, while tearing up a pair of pants which had been the property of a prisoner who had died, found four hundred dollars in greenbacks carefully stitched in the waist of the pants. Of course this was regarded as a large haul — equal to $16,000 of Confederate promises — for every dollar of Uncle Sam's money would buy forty of the money of the waning Confederacy.

One day I got myself into a serious difficulty by buying a blanket belonging to a fellow prisoner in our ward of the hospital. He came to me and insisted on my buying his blanket and continued to press me so persistently that I at last bought it to accommodate him, and not that I needed it particularly. Knowing that orders existed prohibiting the sale and purchase of such articles, I feared I would get into trouble by so doing, but he promised me faithfully that he would never divulge the name of the purchaser under any circumstances. I bought it and paid him his price for it.

About three days later some of the convalescents of our ward, the sixteenth, were being transferred to the eighteenth, and among them was the man who had sold me the blanket. The officials went around gathering the blankets of the patients who were being moved. In this I foresaw trouble, so rolling my three blankets up I went with them down to the eighteenth ward and left them there with a friend with whom I had been interested in trading. Then returning to my tent I awaited events.

I had not long to wait, for having gone for the man who had sold me the blanket they had frightened him into telling to whom he had sold it, and bringing him to my tent he pointed me out as the man who had violated the rules. I was soundly abused in language more forcible than eloquent, and was then told that if I did not produce the blanket and restore it to the owner I would be tied up by the thumbs. Edwards, who was interested in my safety, advised me to confess, but as I had come into possession of the blanket honestly I concluded to hold out, for a while at least.

Failing to accomplish their purpose by threats, I was taken under guard to headquarters for punishment. The major commanding was not in, but a lieutenant who was temporarily in charge said he had no doubts but that it would be in accordance with the orders of the major to tie me up, and it was done. A half-inch rope was procured and fastened to each wrist. Then I was stretched up against an oak tree which stood in front of the major's tent, leaving my feet dangling about a foot from the ground.

I had been hanging in this manner five or ten minutes — long minutes — and was about concluding to loosen my grip on the blanket, the possession of which was the cause of my present painful suspension, when the major returned and at once inquired into the facts of the case. He was informed that I had bought a blanket from a sick comrade and refused to return it when ordered. The major asked me what I had done with the blanket, and I told him that being hungry I had sold it for something to eat. This statement was not as truthful as it might have been, but it served such a good purpose that I never afterward apologized to the officer for telling it, nor have I ever done penance for it. He ordered me taken down and untied, reprimanding the lieutenant severely for his hasty action in the matter, and saying that almost anyone would do the same thing under such circumstances.

The major's conduct in this matter impressed me favorably.[17] I was returned to my quarters and liberated. I afterward took possession of the blanket on account of which I had narrowly escaped severe punishment, and both Edwards and I joined in a season of congratulation over the favorable termination of the affair.

Not long after this occurrence the man with whom I had left the blankets for safekeeping came to me and said that he saw a chance of escape, and desired I should join him in the effort. I told him that if his plan was a feasible one I would share in the adventure, though my experience in that line of exploits had not been full of reward.

I have previously stated that on the south side of the hospital grounds was an extended shallow swamp. On this side the guards walked on the inside of the fence and on the other three sides they walked on the outside. On the south side I noticed that the sentinels were less vigilant at times than the nature of their duties required. They would build little fires on the guard line at night, around which they would stand or sit in couples or singly when they knew that they were not watched by the officers, and at such times the prisoners would approach the guards and traffic with them. In the southeast corner of the grounds a tree which grew on the inside had fallen across the fence and partially knocked it down, the top of the tree falling in the swamp on the outside.

It seemed an easy thing after dark, when the guards were not watching, for a person to crawl over the body of the tree, let himself down into the swamp and escape, and this was the plan by which we hoped to gain our liberty. We hardly hoped to succeed entirely, but we argued that if we could but succeed in scaling the prison fence at this tree and gain temporary freedom of a few days, the effort was worth making and we determined to try it.

We knew that four savage bloodhounds were kept for the purpose of pursuing escaped prisoners, but this fact did not check our determination to see how it looked out in the country. We thought it might be several days before we were missed, and by that time it would be impossible to track us by the scent. We made everything ready to carry out our plan on a certain night. I said nothing to Edwards of our plan for I well knew that he would refuse to go, and would do all he could to prevent my going.

On two different nights we approached the place intending to make the effort, but both times we found the guards unusually watchful and we waited for a more favorable time. On the third night circumstances seemed better and about ten o'clock we crept cautiously down toward the place through which we intended escaping. The guards were standing around a small fire engaged in trading with a number of prisoners. It was cloudy and rain was falling in a gentle shower. The guards seemed to have no fear of anyone trying to make an escape on such a night as this. We saw that no more favorable opportunity than this could be expected, and that if we ever intended making the effort, now was our time.

My partner, whose name was Williams, crept over the log in advance of me and told me to follow. We used the utmost caution, for even the breaking of a twig might arouse the guards. We crept along the trunk of the tree, Williams four feet in advance. Our position at this moment was critical in the extreme, for if discovered we were almost sure to be shot down. But at last we got on the outside. Williams let himself down into the shallow water without making any noise, but when I attempted to do the same thing I slipped and fell into the water with a noisy splash. This raised an alarm. The guards shouted "halt" and opened a brisk fire. But there was very little danger in their firing as the fence was now between us and them, and if it had been open day they could not have fired on us with anything like fatal effect.

I sprang to my feet and got away as fast as possible, never thinking of Williams or of making an effort to keep with him. The swamp abounded with underbrush and old, decaying logs, and was altogether a place through which one could move with very little speed, especially in the darkness.

In my haste to escape I scratched my face and hands and bruised myself in a fearful manner. I stumbled over old logs and many times fell headlong into the mud and water until I was so fatigued I could make no further progress. Halting to rest, I thought of Williams and listened attentively that I might hear him making his way through the swamp. I would have hallooed, but was fearful of being heard by the guards who might possibly be pursuing.

Nothing could be heard of my adventurous comrade, nor did I ever afterward learn of his fate. He was a man of nerve and had a heart as big as all outdoors, and I deeply regretted parting with him, especially at a time like this.

I rested for a long time and continued to hope to hear something from Williams, but in vain. All was quiet except that frogs and other occupants of the swamp made noisy complaints at being disturbed at this hour of the night. I was now filled with fearful apprehensions. I imagined alligators lying in wait to devour me and my situation was such that I began to wish myself back in the prison. Failing to hear from Williams I moved on with great difficulty, hardly knowing whither I went. I had no knowledge of the extent of the swamp and very little knowledge of the direction I was going.

I kept going, thinking I would come out somewhere. About three o'clock in the morning I struck higher ground and realized that I had emerged from the swamp. Here I laid down to rest, and being completely tired out I fell asleep and slept till after daylight. A dense forest surrounded me. Behind me was the swamp and in front and on either hand was an unbroken wilderness of woods.

I had lost all hope of hearing from Williams. I ate a scanty breakfast from the little store of provisions with which I had provided myself before starting. Then resuming my journey I traveled in a southwestern direction through a level and heavily timbered country. I felt all the time that I must emerge into some cultivated and inhabited region, though how I would proceed or what plan I would adopt to secure my escape had not entered my mind. The injuries I had sustained in floundering through the swamp made me stiff and sore and hindered my progress very much.

Finally, about three o'clock in the afternoon, I came in sight of a cultivated plantation, the view of which gave me great joy. I seated myself on a log to rest and after a short time I thought I heard the baying of a dog behind me. I listened with breathless attention and again heard the same sound with more distinctness. I was now convinced that I was being pursued and that the hounds were on my trail. What was to be done? I looked about me and began to plan for the best and to escape the jaws of the hounds, which would soon be upon me. The fork of a tree which stood nearby invited me, so I climbed the trunk and was soon in the fork awaiting the arrival of my pursuers. The dogs, four in number, came up and began barking with savage vigor. Being fifteen feet from the ground I was beyond their reach, and from my perch of safety I contemplated their noisy rage with no little interest.

In a short time three Confederates appeared on horseback. One of them accosted me with "Ah, Yank, we've got you this time." Another called on me to come down at once. I told them to get off their horses and keep the dogs from injuring me and I would come down. One of them dismounted and, driving the dogs back, stood at the tree while I descended. The hounds did not seem inclined to injure me after this.

I was ordered to mount behind one of the men, and the chase being ended we rode in the direction of the prison. As we proceeded they inquired how many had made their escape and also the manner in which it was effected. I told them a straight story and made inquiry concerning Williams, to which they replied that he had not been retaken and they cared very little whether he was or not. These men seemed to be jovial and good-hearted; they chatted socially and treated me in the kindest manner. They expressed themselves as being heartily tired of the war and their general conduct was in marked contrast with that of the guards who had retaken me when I escaped at Danville.

We reached the prison about sundown and I ascertained that I had not reached a point more than seven miles from our place of escape, but must have been traveling in a zigzag course. Upon our arrival I was taken to headquarters and reported to the major commanding. This officer asked me how many escaped with me and by what means we got away. I told him the whole truth, and he believed it. He said that owing to my bruised and battered condition and the rough time I had had in the swamp that he would let me off for this time, but he advised me not to repeat the attempt as it would be impossible to gain my liberty, even if I was successful in escaping from the grounds.

My pitiable condition, hair matted with mud, clothes torn and my face scratched and bruised, presented a plea for clemency stronger than could have been made by the tongue of eloquence. The major in dismissing and sending me to my quarters advised me to take better care of myself, a bit of advice which I accepted thankfully. Shortly after this incident the major was assigned to duty elsewhere and left us, a circumstance which we had cause to regret. He was a man of many excellent qualities and inflicted no unnecessary pain upon the prisoners under him. His whole soul seemed overflowing with the milk of human kindness, and it was a common remark that so good a man was unfortunate in espousing so bad a cause.

I never heard of Williams after our separation in the swamp. He was not captured and returned to the prison or hospital at Andersonville, and his fate remains a mystery to me. The swamp was many miles in extent in one direction, and he may have penetrated deeper and deeper into it and then perished of hunger. Or he may have been killed in being retaken. It is barely possible that by good fortune he succeeded in reaching the lines of our army and was safe. If living, I hope that fate may place this account before him and acquaint him of my whereabouts. I have, somehow, a hope that he still lives.

Events of no very exciting moment occupied our time from this till about the middle of the following January, 1865. I had continued my traffic in various ways, and by so doing managed to scrape together a tolerably good living. The stockade had been unoccupied for almost two months, but by the above named time three or four thousand prisoners were brought in and placed in the stockade, and many, including myself, were sent to the stockade from the hospital.[18] Here we began to retaste some of the horrors of our imprisonment of the preceding summer, but we were not so crowded as before, for instead of 25,000 as formerly we only numbered a little less than 4,000; therefore we had plenty of room. But our rations were scant and it was as much as we could do to live on what we got.

Sometime in the latter part of February five hundred of our number were ordered to move. I was among that number and indulged strongly in the hope of an exchange and release.

A short time previous to this the Confederates had been making efforts to enlist prisoners in the stockade to serve in the Southern army. A Colonel O'Neil, an Irishman of the C.S.A., came into the stockade and succeeded in enlisting some of the stoutest and hardiest of the prisoners.[19] Of those thus enlisted the larger portion were foreigners. None but the very stoutest were taken. I learned afterward that all these deserted in a body and joined the Union army, but this may not be true.

None of those who enlisted should be blamed or censured for using any and every means to obtain their freedom, and I think that each of those who enlisted had strong reasons for doing so, for "all that a man hath will he give for his life." Many persons who stayed at home viewing the war from afar, knowing nothing of the dreadful carnage of battle and experiencing nothing of the horrors of starvation in prison, are the first and loudest to proclaim that they would have died before they would have enlisted thus. Such folks seldom die in this manner.

The order to move, before mentioned, was not carried out immediately, and it was not till the early days of March that we began to pack our scanty effects preparatory to moving out. This was a task to which we applied ourselves with promptness. Shout after shout went up from the men whose hearts had been bowed down with unutterable woe for many weary months. The news seemed almost too good to be true; we found ourselves inquiring of each other whether it was a fact that we had received such orders, or was it a trick of our captors to add one more woe to the long roll of miseries that had embittered our lives. But after some further waiting five hundred of us were marched out of the stockade and to the depot. Our star of hope began to rise and the prospect of release from our charnel-house of horrors began to grow bright. Now that we were out of the hated pen and waiting for a train seemed almost like heaven begun below.

We waited at the depot from 11 a.m. till 4 p.m., and no train coming for us we were again returned to the stockade. What a mighty reverse this was to our feelings — how it blasted the cherished hopes of a few hours before. Our hearts sank within us and dark despair took the place where hope had triumphed but an hour earlier. Many gave up and sank under this blow of disappointment. Tears were shed and maledictions and curses were heard on every hand. It was like snatching the cooling water from the victim of consuming thirst. Many said that we may as well make up our minds to die in prison and no longer cherish hopes which budded but to perish. And in this state of hopelessness many did die. We resumed our places in the stockade and knew not what the future promised.

About two weeks after this [April 4, 1865], orders were again received and again the fires of hope were kindled within us. This order was greeted with an outburst of joy which baffles description. Our labor of packing up and preparing to move was speedily and cheerfully performed. This being completed we marched with light hearts to the depot, finding a train of box cars in waiting. We were soon aboard and were much crowded, but we were so overjoyed at the prospect of leaving that we cared little for the discomfort we experienced.

Our train moved in a southerly direction, running as far as Albany in the southern part of Georgia. Here this line of railroad terminated. We were now fifty miles from Andersonville. It was after dark when we reached Albany. We were taken from the cars and laid by till next morning.

Rations were issued to us in the morning and we were told we were now on the way to the Union lines, and that this supply of food must last us till we reached our friends. We were so overjoyed at the prospect of gaining our liberty that we now cared very little about what was given us to eat.

From this place we took up a line of march, and for three days we traveled in a southeasterly direction through a level country and over what I considered very poor soil. We marched about twenty miles a day, and at the close of the third day reached Thomasville, the seat of Thomas County, one of the border counties of Georgia on the Florida line. Our sick were hauled across the country from Albany in wagons. Many men gave out on the march and they, too, were hauled. It became necessary to press into service the teams and wagons of planters living along the line of march, and by so doing our transportation was made equal to our needs.

At Thomasville we received some kind attentions which I mention with pleasure, and which show that even in an enemy's land we were treated as if we were human in character at least. On the day after our arrival many ladies visited us, bringing baskets full of provisions, daintily prepared, and distributed them to the sick and most destitute of our number. They brought many articles of clothing and gave to those in need. Many a sick and dying prisoner invoked God's blessing on the heads of these angels of mercy as they ministered among us. This incident was like a gleam of sunshine on a dark day, like a spring of water in a thirsty land.

On the next day we were told that owing to a lack of cars we could not leave till the following day. And on the next day and for several successive days we were told the same comfortless story. These delays seemed ominous of nothing good. Rumors of various kinds floated through the camp and our star of hope began to lose its brilliancy. Many of us prophesied that evil was near at hand and the most hopeful began to doubt. Even our guards seemed confused and hardly knew what to do with us or themselves.

Thus time wore on till the fifth day, when we were ordered to be ready to move. But instead of marching us to the depot and a train as we had hoped, we were turned back and marched in the direction of Albany on the same road over which we had marched with such buoyant hearts and bright hopes but a few days before. At this unhappy turn in our affairs, who can describe the despair which weighed down every heart, for we seemed to see and understand in this movement that our cup of sorrow was not yet drained of all its galling bitterness. We would a hundredfold sooner have marched in any other direction than toward Andersonville. How we hated, loathed and detested the very name of the spot where we had seen and suffered so much. And now, after having our hopes raised to such a point that we could almost see the stars and stripes of the dear old flag, and hear the anthems of liberty, and taste the joys of freedom — now that we were made to turn our backs on all this and march toward our hated prison-pen, the thought was crushing and next to death itself.

Heavy hearts make heavy feet; we were four days reaching Albany. We were sick, weary, disheartened and the last ray of hope was almost extinguished. At Albany we were put on the cars and in a brief time were again within the walls of dreary Andersonville. If we had been sad and disheartened in counter-marching toward our old place of torment, how much more forlorn and dejected did we now feel in realizing that hope had fled and despair held a heartless mastery. Nothing could be learned concerning the progress of the war and our knowledge of the outside world was almost a blank.

Most of us bore our misfortunes as stoically as possible and determined to keep our spirits up to the end. But how we succeeded in doing so seems almost marvel. The actions of our captors seemed to indicate that they considered their cause a hopeless one, and in this we drew a little comfort.

At the end of about ten days after our return from Thomasville we again received orders to move, and once again we gathered together our scanty effects, hoping in this, our third moving, to see the last of Andersonville. We marched to the depot and got aboard a train of cars a little after dark. We noticed that our guards were much excited over some news which we construed to be in our favor, and they seemed to care very little whether we escaped or not and made little effort to prevent escape. I saw more than one opportunity of escaping, but I began to realize that we were a burden on their hands and that they were becoming every hour more and more anxious of getting rid of us.

Our train moved out at ten o'clock p.m., but instead of going south as before, we moved in the direction of Macon. This was as we wished, for we felt more hope of getting into our lines in this direction than by going south. We were all night and till eight o'clock the next day running to Macon, a distance of sixty miles. Captain Wirz accompanied the train, and he seemed considerably excited over something which he kept to himself. When the train halted at Macon the captain passed from one car to another, assuring the men that this time they would certainly be sent through to the Union lines, and he seemed more like a man and less like the fiend that he was than on any former occasion. We regarded this as an item in our favor.

We remained at Macon nearly two hours, during which time we stayed in the cars, and then again we were run back toward Andersonville.[20] Who can imagine our feelings as the train sped in the direction of the place we most detested on earth. We asked each other, "Shall we never be free from this horrid place?" We reached Andersonville at three o'clock in the afternoon, but contrary to our expectations, and to our agreeable surprise, we were not allowed to leave the train and were assured that after a short halt we would be sent on. This announcement was cheered lustily. The poor sufferers shook hands, shed tears and made many demonstrations of the joy which filled their hearts. The scene was one which cannot be described.

After a halt of half an hour our train again moved, going south. We reached Albany at nine o'clock that night and, disembarking, spent the remainder of the night. In the morning we had issued to us six hardtack which were to feed us for three days. We then set out to march to Thomasville, which place we reached at the end of three days' marching. Such of our numbers as could not be transported in wagons were left at Albany, and afterward sent forward.

On the day following our arrival at Thomasville we were again put on board a train. Serious apprehensions harassed us and again doubts filled our minds, for we were yet ignorant of our destination. *But we were going away from Andersonville.* There was a world of comfort in that. Our course for sixteen or twenty hours seemed to be a zigzag one, but at the end of that time we reached Lake City in Florida. Here we went into camp at a distance of four miles from the city. Our camp was beside the railroad and near a pond of stagnant water, from which we supplied ourselves with water to use and drink. We at length found plenty of better water by digging four or five feet.

Some of the men were wading in the pond a short distance from the bank when they came across a young alligator six feet in length. They set about trying to kill it with clubs. The guards, attracted by the confusion, came to their assistance and the alligator was shot, after which the carcass was cut up and divided among us. We had been so long without meat that we thought we could eat anything; besides, we were on the verge of starvation. All the rations we had received since leaving Albany were a half dozen crackers and a small quantity of meal. In the distribution of the alligator the mess to which I belonged got the tail. This we skinned and cut into thin slices, after which it was boiled and eaten. Under the circumstances we agreed the meat was as good as any we had ever tasted.

We remained in camp near Lake City four days, then boarding a train we were sent to Baldwin, a small place about forty miles in an easterly direction. This was an outpost of the Confederate army at this time in the direction of Jacksonville, where a part of our army was stationed. The railroad to Jacksonville had been destroyed by one or both armies, and this station was as far as the cars were running in the direction of the Union lines.

From Baldwin to Jacksonville was sixteen miles, and we were told that we were to reach it on foot. We had been guarded from Andersonville to this place by a regiment of infantry commanded by a Colonel Gibbs. We left Baldwin at ten o'clock in the morning and marched in the direction of Jacksonville. Our guards accompanied us a few miles when the colonel called a halt. He told us that his command would go no farther, that we were now at liberty, and by pursuing our way along the railroad we would soon reach our forces at Jacksonville in safety. He advised us to assist each other on the march and keep together as well as we could. He assured us that we would find our friends ready to receive us at Jacksonville. He and his command then bade us good-bye and turned back. I do not remember that any tears of regret were shed on the occasion.

And now such joyous shouts and prolonged cheers as went up from this haggard crowd of famished men seldom is heard by mortal ears. The fact that we were within a few miles of the flag which we had so long a desire to see seemed to be a joy almost purer than we could bear.

As soon as our guards left us all order of march was at an end, and each man set out and moved ahead to suit himself regardless of his stronger or weaker companion. In a short time the line was lengthened out to a distance of more than two miles. I marched as well as I could, but soon fell behind the majority; yet, as far backward as I could see there were many stragglers all trying their best to make the desired end.

I was barefooted and hatless. My breeches were worn off to the knees and my shirt had lost its sleeves. All the baggage I had was half of an old blanket which I threw over my shoulders when it rained. Many marched until they became exhausted and then sank beside the way. My feet were blistered, swollen and full of prickles from sand burs. I kept on, doing my best till three o'clock in the afternoon, when I dropped beside the road feeling that I must rest, for though liberty beckoned and freedom glittered ahead of me, the flesh was weaker than the will. I rested for more than an hour and during that time many of the stragglers came up and passed on. Yet there were many more who were still in the rear.

As I again moved on, an old man came hobbling along and seemed to be exerting his utmost to get ahead. As he walked by my side I noticed his labored breathing. Suddenly he fell forward on his face. I stopped and gave him some attention. One or two other soldiers came up and, while we were discussing what was best to do with him, he ceased to breathe. He lived not more than six minutes after he fell. We then moved on, leaving the lifeless body where it had fallen. I was informed that many in the rear were lying unable to get farther.

About sundown we came to a picket post of our army in the vicinity of Jacksonville. I had not felt free until I was well inside the lines of our army, for I did not know but the wheel of fate would yet make an unfortunate turn and we should again fall into the hands of the enemy.

I entered Jacksonville in the dusk of the evening, and as I passed along a street I saw a colored woman carrying half of a large fish. I begged a portion of it off her and carried it into camp for my supper. It was fully dark when I found my comrades in camp. Wagonloads of light bread were issued to us after our arrival, with barrels of good coffee as an accompaniment. This and the fish furnished me such a supper as I had not had in an age.

Next day a force was sent out to bring in those prisoners who had become exhausted on the march. I was told that five poor fellows had died on the march, and I know of many others, nearly forty, who died soon after reaching Jacksonville. The excitement of again being free had caused many to over-exert their strength, and the frail tenement gave way.

It was now April 28th, 1865. I had been taken at Chickamauga, September 20th, 1863, making my imprisonment nineteen months and eight days.[21] I am safe in saying that there are not now living, of all the thousands who suffered as prisoners of war, fifty men who served for the length of time I did. And, if there is any horror in all the long lists of sickness, starvation and untold misery which fell to the lot of any of my fellow prisoners, and which I did not suffer, it must be too dreadful to be told.

At Jacksonville we learned that the war was about ended, that President Lincoln had been killed, and that many other matters of public interest had transpired of which we had been ignorant. We remained a month longer at Jacksonville and during that time more of our number died. Many who were unable to control themselves ate too greedily, and not a few caused their own deaths in this manner.

From Jacksonville we were taken by hospital boat to Annapolis, Maryland. Here we learned of the capture of Jeff. Davis and that the war was ended.[22] New clothing was issued to us and we received the money due us for rations during our imprisonment. This was twenty-five cents a day for each day of our captivity.

From Annapolis we were sent to Camp Chase near Columbus.[23]

Remaining here one night I next day took the train for my home at Carysville, Ohio, where I arrived about noon. I had long been regarded by my friends as dead, and my appearance among them was as one from the grave.

This is my story of prison life. I have made no effort to overdraw the facts in any part of it, but have told the truth. I may have stated inaccuracies regarding dates, distances, names and other minor matters, but my description of the suffering and starvation in the prisons where I suffered is short of the truth, in that the worst cannot be told. If the living could not speak, there are the graves of an army of martyrs at Andersonville which tell the story better than my feeble pen has done.[24]

In thus giving to the public this simple narrative, I am actuated by no desire to stir up strife or to engender bitter feelings toward any section of our now happy country, for I believe that all feelings of bitterness should be buried in the grave of forgetfulness. Let us cherish a love for our dear country and its institutions, the preservation and perpetuation of which has cost so much blood and sacrifice. And in the language of our country's great founder, let us "frown indignantly upon the first dawning of any attempt to alienate any portion of our country from the rest, or to enfeeble the sacred ties that now link together the various parts."

It is a source of regret to me that the fortunes of war placed me where I did not share in the crimson glory which the 113th O.V.I. won on so many well-fought fields, and that the associations I had formed among the membership of the dear old command should terminate as they did, never to be renewed again until the final reveille that shall awake the heroic.

Yours,

J.N. Hall

Andersonville Notes

1. Soon to be known as Andersonville prison, Camp Sumter was established early in 1864 to help relieve overcrowding in Richmond and Danville, its remote location in southwest central Georgia thought to be safe from Federal attack. On February 24, 1864, the first Union prisoners arrived at Andersonville from Richmond's Belle Isle prison camp. [Speer, 259; William Marvel, *Andersonville: The Last Depot* (Chapel Hill: The University of North Carolina Press, 1994), p. 27].

2. Born Hartmann Heinrich Wirz on November 25, 1823, in Zurich, Switzerland, Captain Henry Wirz was vilified by nearly every Union prisoner known to have written about captivity at Andersonville. An 1849 émigré to the United States, he lived in Massachusetts, Kentucky and Louisiana prior to the Civil War. In 1862 Wirz was assigned to the staff of General John H. Winder, who placed him in command of Camp Sumter's (Andersonville's) prison stockade in early March 1864. As Union prisoners there began dying by the thousands, Northern newspapers characterized both Wirz and Winder as "inhuman fiends" and "monsters." After the war Wirz was tried by Federal authorities for murder, abuse of prisoners and conspiracy to murder prisoners en masse. Among modern-day historians, Arch Fredric Blakey has written: "There is no question that Wirz did not receive a fair trial. Testimony by men who were not even at Andersonville was routine, accusations that he committed murder when he was not even there were accepted as unimpeachable facts, and he was not allowed to have anyone testify for his defense. Still, Wirz was not a likable figure; by all accounts he was rough, profane, and hot-tempered, and no one could deny the horrors of Andersonville." Pronounced guilty, he was hanged in Washington's Old Capitol Prison yard on November 10, 1865. At the time of his death Wirz was two weeks shy of his 42nd birthday. [John A. Garraty & Mark C. Carnes, editors, *American National Biography*, vol. 23 (New York: Oxford University Press, Inc., 1999), p. 679-680].

3. This stream was a branch of the incongruously named Sweetwater Creek. Most prisoners came to call it "Stockade Creek."

4. Prisoner-of-war memoranda in Hall's compiled service record do not provide a specific date of his arrival at Andersonville.

5. Andersonville's most prominent dealer was James Selman Jr., a prison staff clerk whose lean-to sutler shanty stood just inside the stockade's north gate. Selman, whose prices were among the prison's highest, periodically offered watermelons, muskmelons, cucumbers, onions, potatoes, wheat, flour, coffee, sugar, salt, fowl and seafood. With very little money remaining in the

prison by autumn of 1864, Selman closed his sutlery at the end of September. [Marvel, p. 48, 108, 212].

6. The death of Adam Swarner was the first recorded at Andersonville on February 27, 1864. Swarner, age 25, mustered into Company H, 2nd New York Cavalry, as a corporal in August 1861. Captured at Liberty Mills, Va.,

Orderly Sergeant Horace B. Smith, Company B, 82nd Ohio, was among the first 50 Union prisoners to lose their lives at Andersonville. Wounded and captured July 1, 1863, at the battle of Gettysburg, he was confined six months on Belle Isle in Richmond before transfer to Camp Sumter's stockade. Just three weeks later, on March 14, 1864, the 20-year-old native of Newark, Ohio, died of typhoid fever in the prison hospital. Grave #44 in Andersonville National Cemetery contains his remains.

Richard W. Fink Collection

on September 22, 1863, he was confined at Richmond's Belle Isle a week later and sent to Andersonville with the first batch of prisoners. Belonging to the same company and regiment, Swarner's brother Jacob was captured in October 1863 near Warrenton, Va., and arrived at Andersonville the following March. On July 26, 1864, he died there as well. [Marvel, p. 28; *Annual Report of the Adjutant-General of the State of New York For the Year 1893,* vol. II (Albany: James B. Lyon, State Printer, 1894), p. 662].

7. In actuality, a 10-acre addition to the stockade's north end enlarged the prison to 26 and a half acres. The addition was completed June 30, 1864, and opened the next day. [Speer, p. 259, 261].

8. In July 1862 a cartel was reached for an immediate and general exchange of prisoners, but it broke down 10 months later when an "insurmountable stalemate" developed between the warring governments, primarily over repatriation of black Union soldiers and their white commanding officers. In April

1864, General Ulysses S. Grant ordered no further prisoner exchanges until the Confederates balanced Federal releases. That August he again refused to exchange enemy prisoners, expressing a belief that such exchanges would prolong the war. Grant relented in January 1865, however, and exchanges were duly reinstituted. [Speer, p. 102-105; E.B. Long, *The Civil War Day by Day: An Almanac 1861-1865* (Garden City, N.Y.: Doubleday & Company, Inc., 1971), p. 486, 557, 628].

9. The court sat *inside* the stockade's south gate enclosure, and the defendants were brought in singly to confront their accusers. [Marvel, p. 100].

10. The Catholic priest was Father Peter Whelan, 62, of Savannah, Ga. He ministered devotedly to Andersonville's inmates from June 16 to the first of October 1864. [Marvel, p. 140-141].

11. Within days of Atlanta's fall to Union troops under General William T. Sherman, the Confederates began transferring Andersonville prisoners by rail to other less threatened locations in Georgia and South Carolina. The first detachments left September 7, 1864, and by the 13th fewer than 16,000 men remained in the stockade. [Marvel, p. 198-199, 202].

12. Hall's mortality figure is inflated. According to prison consolidated morning reports, the following numbers of deaths were recorded for selected dates: July 9 — 42; July 10 — 56; July 11 — 38; August 1 through 4 — an average of 74 per day; August 5 — 90; and August 6 — 103, the first time more than 100 men died within a single 24-hour period. In August, Andersonville's all-time population high of nearly 33,000 made it, in effect, the fifth largest "city" in the Confederacy. [Marvel, p. 286, 169; Speer, p. 262].

13. Beginning in August 1864 and continuing into September, four narrow, two-story wooden barracks buildings were constructed along the stockade's northern wall. Roofed with boards, the barracks had no walls due to a shortage of nails. They resembled livestock sheds and each could accommodate 270 men. [Marvel, p. 192].

14. According to Hall's POW records' memoranda, he was admitted to Andersonville's hospital on September 13, 1864.

Private Amos P. Flowers, 95th Ohio, had known Hall since 1859 and was a fellow prisoner at Andersonville for several months following his capture at Brice's Crossroads, Miss., on June 10, 1864. A quarter century later Flowers stated that Hall "was then [September 1864] suffering from scurvy of the mouth. I could have pulled his teeth out with my fingers, or they seemed loose enough to have done that. I know he suffered also from hunger and like a great many [others] more or less suffered from diarrhoea." [A.P. Flowers deposition in J.N. Hall pension application, claim #610254, RG 15, NARA].

15. Sergeant John Edwards of Company H, 90th Pennsylvania, was a 29-year-old upholsterer born in Philadelphia. A veteran volunteer, he had been captured May 5, 1864, during the battle of the Wilderness in Virginia. Edwards died at Florence, S.C., on February 10, 1865, of scurvy "contracted from ill treatment."

Born in Germany, Private August H. Schrader, Company I, 112th Illinois, was a 24-year-old farmer upon enlistment in August 1862. Captured September 26, 1863, near Riceville, Tenn., he first was confined in Richmond, then Danville and finally Andersonville. His admittance to Andersonville's hospital (for scurvy) was dated July 16, 1864, and he remained there until January 10, 1865. Schrader was paroled April 28, 1865, at Jacksonville, Fla. [J. Edwards and A.H. Schrader compiled service records, RG 94, NARA].

16. Of 1,359 men in the hospital wards December 1, 1864, 116 died during the next three weeks. [Marvel, p. 225].

17. The identity of this officer is unclear, but the major may have belonged to either the 2nd Georgia Reserves or 55th Georgia Infantry, portions of which composed Andersonville's guard force at the time. Since October 9, 1864, Colonel George C. Gibbs had been post commander at Camp Sumter. [Marvel, p. 215, 219].

18. On November 11, 1864, the last 841 inmates were removed from Andersonville's stockade. It remained empty until December 22, when a thousand Union prisoners from camps at Blackshear and Thomasville, Ga., were herded through the stockade's gates. By the day after Christmas 3,000 more had arrived. [Marvel, p. 220, 227-228].

Hall's memoranda of POW records state he was released from the hospital December 27, 1864, and returned to the stockade the next day.

19. Colonel John G. O'Neill, 10th Tennessee Infantry, had enlisted about 250 such "Galvanized Yankees" at Camp Lawton prison in Millen, Ga., before visiting Andersonville November 15-16, 1864. His recruiting effort there produced only eight volunteers from among the camp's hospital or paroled prisoners. The following February, however, recruiters successfully lured 138 desperate Andersonville prisoners to the Confederate army. [Marvel, p. 223, 234].

20. This incident occurred April 18, 1865. Two days previous, Union Brevet Major General James H. Wilson's cavalry corps occupied Columbus and West Point, Ga., before veering toward Macon, which the Federal horsemen reached April 20. Their close presence had forced the trains carrying Hall and his fellow prisoners to turn back south. [*Official Records,* series I, vol. XLIX, pt. 1, p. 340, 365-366].

21. Hall was paroled April 28, 1865, the first full day after he arrived in Jacksonville.

22. Hall reported May 29 at College Green Barracks in Annapolis. That same day, President Andrew Johnson granted amnesty and pardon to all persons who directly or indirectly participated in "the existing rebellion," with a number of exceptions. Included among these were all those who allegedly mistreated prisoners of war.

The Confederacy's president, Jefferson Davis, had been taken into custody May 10, 1865, by Federal cavalry near Irwinville, Ga. [J.N. Hall compiled service record, RG 94, NARA; Long, p. 687, 690-691].

23. Hall left Annapolis June 8, 1865, and reached Camp Chase in Ohio two days later.

24. Of roughly 41,000 Union soldiers who were incarcerated at Andersonville between February 1864 and April 1865, 12,913 died. Andersonville National Cemetery's prisoner burial ground contains 13,714 graves, of which 921 are marked unknown.

5

Epilogue

Having marched triumphantly down Washington's Pennsylvania Avenue during May 1865's Grand Review parade, the 113th Ohio traveled by train and steamboat to Louisville, Kentucky, where it was addressed by General William T. Sherman, received its last pay and mustered out of service July 6. On the 8th, 487 officers and men of the regiment reached Columbus, Ohio, where, two afternoons later, many of them attended "a fine collation spread upon the tables" at Goodale Park. "Our citizens seemed to make amends for former neglect," noted a local newspaperman, "and were out in full force. This was especially true in reference to the ladies, more of them being present ... than at any other five receptions tendered our returning soldiers." [1]

Jasper Hall, however, was not among his old comrades enjoying the "bounteous" supper and encomiums delivered by a half dozen speakers. A month previous his own homecoming had taken place 53 miles to the west in Carysville, where he was reunited with his young wife, family and friends. When they last saw him Hall was 160 pounds; now, painfully emaciated, he weighed barely 94. Understandably, everyone he knew was shocked at his appearance and condition.

"He looked terrible," recalled Carysville resident Amos Flowers, a fellow Andersonville prisoner who made it home three months earlier. Another neighbor, Jesse F. Halterman, had spent five weeks with Hall in Andersonville, and was among those transferred from the stockade in September 1864 who left him in what was thought the near throes of death. "I distinctly remember," Halterman testified, "that he was badly affected with scurvy, that his gums were inflamed, sore and rotting away, and his teeth loose. His legs were much swollen to the knees, and the skin, especially along the shin bone, discolored black. ... When I last visited him and told him good bye he was lying on the ground helpless, without shelter of any kind, unable to rise, but held up his hand to me. I did not expect ever to see him again alive." Between 1865 and 1868, Halterman encountered Hall "every few days and frequently alluded to our prison experience, and it has always been a matter of surprise to me that [he] survived."[2]

Rockwell Seely had been back in Carysville more than a year before Hall's return. Seely also had fought at Chickamauga, soldiering on in the 113th Ohio in spite of "age" (he was nearly 51), until several debilitating factors forced his own discharge in February 1864. His son-in-law "was badly broken down when he arrived at home," the shoemaker recollected. "He was very much afflicted and so poor [in health] that he did not resemble J.N.H. at all, having scurvy very bad. I thought every tooth in his head was loose." Hall's wife, Florence, stated more succinctly: "He came home from the army very sick."[3]

Although fathering four children over the next five years, Hall remained physically weak as he attempted to resume teaching. Rheumatism wracked both legs (a cane aided walking), and he frequently endured bouts with diarrhea. In search of a "healthier" place to live, he moved his growing family by way of Panama to the Pacific Northwest late in 1868. A younger brother and sister already were residing there. But according to Florence, Hall did "nothing much for a long time after we went to Oregon." Manual labor was nearly impossible. "If he had had to go out to work after his return from the army, and as long as I lived with him, he never could have stood it."

Florence averred that her husband always had been "temperate in habits" (a Protestant, he had joined the Masonic fraternity in 1866), but after four or five years in Oregon Hall "became discouraged because he did not [find] such employment as he could follow. [He] got to drinking and for the last 3 years I was there he drank pretty heavily, and this was partly the cause of our separating, and I procured [a] divorce on account of neglect and failure to support."[4]

The Halls' marriage ended in 1880, the same year he likely wrote his prison memoir. By then he'd finally found steady work teaching at Central Point in southwest Oregon's Rogue River valley. Initially built of logs and later of finished lumber, the small community's school was among the first established in Jackson County, and Hall, christened "Professor" by Central Point's inhabitants, was its first teacher. One of his female students recalled many years later that she became Hall's "pet," and each time they crossed paths outside the classroom he gave her fifty cents. When last she saw him he presented her with his photograph.[5]

Hall also taught at the Klamath Indian Agency school before relocating, in 1887, to Myrtle Creek in Douglas County, Oregon. Teaching only provided a $60 per month salary, so, with a willing partner, Hall commenced raising cattle. He simultaneously began an earnest campaign to secure an army pension as well. In the meantime he kept in touch with his children and ex-father-in-law via letters, occasionally traveling to Ohio for visits when school was not in session.[6]

At first the cattle business promised success, but during Oregon's severe winter of 1888-89 disaster struck. Hall and his partner suffered an estimated loss of $30,000 when most of their herd died. From this financial reverse Hall emerged with about $1,700, which he promptly invested in a Colorado mining operation and moved, yet again, to Denver. That sojourn proved short-lived, too. The mining venture failed almost from the beginning, leaving Hall nearly penniless. After disposing of his watch in order to pay a doctor's bill, he returned east once more and by late spring of 1891 was back in Ohio. There, in the Butler County seat of Hamilton, he tried to secure a public schools' teaching position, to no avail. Deeply disappointed, Hall decided to apply for admission to the National Soldiers Home at Dayton. At the age of 56, bereft of employment and drawing a pension of just six dollars a month, the ex-POW entered the Soldiers Home on November 6, 1891. But he brought with him an inestimable measure of consolation: Eighteen days earlier he had married Lillie D. Whiton of New Bedford, Massachusetts, in a civil ceremony at Butler County's courthouse.[7]

Hall's fortunes improved dramatically during the next quarter century he spent in Dayton. A lucrative job was provided him as superintendent of the Soldiers Home annex. Soon afterward he was commissioned an officer and appointed commander of the home's Company 24, composed of 120 veterans. As such he carried the title "Captain" for the rest of his life. An active member of the Grand Army of the Republic, Hall "discharged his official functions in a manner highly creditable to himself and to the satisfaction of the management of the institution."[8]

Having become an octogenarian in 1915 and recently widowed, Hall accepted an invitation to live with his oldest son, John Court-land Hall, a Medford, Oregon, orchard owner and former teacher. On June 20, 1916, at his own request, Hall was discharged from the Soldiers Home and arrived in Oregon July 5. He had just settled in with "Court" and his wife when, in a freak accident during Jackson County fair week that September, he was thrown from a taxi and suffered a comminuted skull fracture. Lying comatose in the city's Sacred Heart Hospital, Hall was unaware of his 81st birthday marked on October 1. Ten days later he passed away and was laid to rest October 12, 1916, in Medford's Eastwood I.O.O.F. cemetery.[9]

Epilogue Notes

1. McAdams, p. 168, 170; *Urbana Citizen and Gazette,* July 13, 1865; *Ohio State Journal,* July 11, 1865.

2. A.P. Flowers and J.F. Halterman depositions in J.N. Hall pension application, claim #610254, RG 15, NARA. A Champaign County farmer, Jesse Halterman was 17 years old upon enlistment in Company B, 20th Ohio Infantry, in August 1861. The veteran volunteer was captured July 22, 1864, at the battle of Atlanta and paroled in North Carolina the following February. [J.F. Halterman compiled service record, RG 94, NARA].

3. R.H. Seely compiled service record, RG 94, NARA; R.H. Seely and F.D. Hall depositions in J.N. Hall pension application, claim #610254, RG 15, NARA. Seely's discharge for disability was dated February 17, 1864, at Tyner's Station, Ga. On March 7, a messmate in Company E, 113th Ohio, wrote home from Rossville, Ga., that 1st Corporal R.H. Seely "has been discharged from the service of the United States on account of old age and debility. Mr. Seely is a man of pure patriotism, high moral character, and upright principles. He participated in the bloody battle of Chickamauga, since which time he has lost his speech entirely. He retires to private life with the respect of all with whom he has braved the dangers of war." [*Ohio Rosters,* vol. VIII, p. 90; *Urbana Citizen and Gazette,* March 17, 1864].

4. Conover, p. 553, 554; F.D. Hall deposition, July 10, 1889, in J.N. Hall pension application. Even before her divorce was finalized, Florence Hall, a seamstress, returned to Ohio and resided in Springfield.

5. J.N. Hall pension file #477895, NARA; *Central Point Times,* January 14, 1965; Joseph G. Follansbee, "Central Point Stories," *Table Rock Sentinel,* vol. 9 (May-June 1989), p. 23.

6. Conover, p. 554; J.N. Hall deposition, June 8, 1889, pension application, claim #610254, RG 15, NARA; J.N. Hall obituary, *The Medford Sun,* October 12, 1916.

7. Conover, p. 554; J.N. Hall National Military Home records, Veterans Administration Medical Center, Dayton, Ohio; J.N. Hall pension file #477895, NARA. Hall's monthly pension increased to $12 in 1892, $14 in 1906, $24 by the end of 1907, and $30 by 1916. He was fully admitted to the Soldiers Home on June 22, 1893.

8. Conover, p. 554. In April 1907, Hall listed his address for the U.S. Pension Bureau as Company 22, National Military Home, Montgomery County, Ohio.

9. J.N. Hall National Military Home records; J. Courtland Hall to U.S.

Pension Bureau, October 22, 1916, in J.N. Hall pension file #477895, NARA; J.N. Hall death certificate, Medford, Jackson County, Ore., October 11, 1916; J.N. Hall obituary, *The Medford Sun,* October 12, 1916.

Bibliography

Compiled service records of volunteer Union soldiers who served in organizations from the states of Ohio, Illinois and Pennsylvania. Records of the Adjutant General's Office, 1780-1917, Record Group 94, National Archives and Records Administration (NARA), Washington, D.C.

Jasper Newton Hall pension files, Record Group 15, NARA.

Jasper Newton Hall National Military Home records, Veterans Administration Medical Center, Dayton, Ohio.

Central Point (Ore.) *Times*
Ohio State Journal
The Medford (Ore.) *Sun*
Richmond (Va.) *Dispatch*
Urbana (Ohio) *Citizen and Gazette*
Urbana (Ohio) *Union*

Bates, Samuel P., *History of Pennsylvania Volunteers, 1861-5,* vol. III, Harrisburg: B. Singerly, State Printer, 1870.

Baumgartner, Richard A., *Buckeye Blood: Ohio at Gettysburg,* Huntington, W.Va.: Blue Acorn Press, 2003.

——, *Blue Lightning: Wilder's Mounted Infantry Brigade in the Battle of Chickamauga,* Huntington, W.Va.: Blue Acorn Press, 2007.

Brook, John P., "His Prison Experience," *The National Tribune,* December 31, 1891.

——, "That Sugar Raid. A Chickamauga Prisoner Gives His Experience," *The National Tribune,* February 19, 1891.

Buslett, Ole A., *Det Femtende Regiment Wisconsin Frivillige,* Decorah, Iowa: B. Amundsen, 1894.

Conover, Frank, editor, *Centennial Portrait and Biographical Record of the City of Dayton and of Montgomery County, Ohio,* Logansport, Ind.: A.W. Bowen & Co., 1897.

Davidson, Henry M., *Fourteen Months in Southern Prisons,* Milwaukee: Daily Wisconsin Printing House, 1865.

Dunlap, George S., "From a Prisoner's Diary," *The National Tribune,* October 15, 1903.

Flack, James T., "In Dreary Old Pemberton," *The National Tribune,* April 18, 1901.

Follansbee, Joseph G., "Central Point Stories," *Table Rock Sentinel,* vol. 9, May-June 1989.

Garraty, John A. & Carnes, Mark C., editors, *American National Biography,* vol. 23, New York: Oxford University Press, Inc., 1999.

Hyde, Solon, *A Captive of War,* edited by Neil Thompson, Shippensburg, Pa.: Burd Street Press, 1996.

Illinois. *Report of the Adjutant General of the State of Illinois,* vol. 6, Springfield: Journal Company Printers, 1900.

"In Richmond. The Great Sugar Raid by Union Prisoners," *The National Tribune,* January 1, 1891.

Isham, Asa B., "Care of Prisoners of War, North and South," *Sketches of War History 1861-1865,* vol. II, Cincinnati: Robert Clarke & Co., 1888.

Jones, B.F., "Rebel Prisons," *The National Tribune,* May 19, 1904.

Long, E.B., *The Civil War Day by Day: An Almanac 1861-1865,* Garden City, N.Y.: Doubleday & Company, Inc., 1971.

Marvel, William, *Andersonville: The Last Depot,* Chapel Hill: The University of North Carolina Press, 1994.

McAdams, Francis M., *Every-Day Soldier Life, or a History of the One Hundred and Thirteenth Ohio Volunteer Infantry,* Columbus: M. Cott & Co., 1884.

McFall, F. Lawrence Jr., *Danville in the Civil War,* Lynchburg, Va.: H.E. Howard, Inc., 2001.

New York. *Annual Report of the Adjutant-General of the State of New York For the Year 1893,* vol. II, Albany: James B. Lyon, State Printer, 1894.

Ohio. Roster Commission. *Official Roster of the Soldiers of the State of Ohio in the War of the Rebellion, 1861-1866,* 12 volumes, Akron, Cincinnati, Norwalk: 1886-1895.

Reid, Whitelaw, *Ohio in the War. Her Statesmen, Generals and Soldiers,* 2 volumes, Cincinnati: The Robert Clarke Company, 1895.

Robertson, James I. Jr., "Houses of Horror: Danville's Civil War Prisons," *The Virginia Magazine of History and Biography,* vol. 69, no. 3, July 1961.

Sneden, Robert Knox, *Eye of the Storm: A Civil War Odyssey,* New York: The Free Press, 2000.

Speer, Lonnie R., *Portals to Hell: Military Prisons of the Civil War,* Mechanicsburg, Pa.: Stackpole Books, 1997.

The History of Champaign County, Ohio, Chicago: W.H. Beers & Co., 1881.

United States War Department. *The War of the Rebellion: A Compilation of the Official Records of the Union and Confederate Armies,* series I and II, Washington: Government Printing Office, 1880-1901.

Waitt, Robert W. Jr., *Confederate Military Hospitals in Richmond,* Richmond: Civil War Centennial Committee, 1964.

Ward, Steven H., *Buckeyes All. A Compendium and Bibliography of Ohio in the Civil War,* vol. V revised, Dayton: privately published, 2004.

Warner, Ezra J., *Generals in Gray: Lives of the Confederate Commanders,* Baton Rouge: Louisiana State University Press, 1959.

Welsh, Jack D., *Medical Histories of Confederate Generals,* Kent, Ohio: Kent State University Press, 1995.

Index

Other books written or edited by Richard A. Baumgartner:

*Blue Lightning: Wilder's Mounted Infantry Brigade
in the Battle of Chickamauga*
(Recipient of the Alexander C. McClurg Award)

Kennesaw Mountain June 1864

Buckeye Blood: Ohio at Gettysburg

Echoes of Battle: The Struggle for Chattanooga

Echoes of Battle: The Atlanta Campaign
(Recipient of the Richard B. Harwell Award)

Yankee Tigers: Through the Civil War with the 125th Ohio

*Yankee Tigers II: Civil War Field Correspondence
from the Tiger Regiment of Ohio*

Blood & Sacrifice: The Civil War Journal of a Confederate Soldier

*The Long Road Home:
Ten Thousand Miles Through the Confederacy with the 68th Ohio*

Fritz: The World War I Memoir of a German Lieutenant

*This Carnival of Hell:
German Combat Experience on the Somme, July–November 1916*

www.BlueAcornPress.com

Blue Acorn Press
P.O. Box 2684 • Huntington, WV 25726 • (304) 733-3917